THE
VOW

THE VOW

**RODNEY & ADONICA
HOWARD-BROWNE**

River Publishing

THE VOW

Copyright © 2024 by Rodney & Adonica Howard-Browne

Unless otherwise noted, all scriptures are from the King James Version (KJV): King James Version, public domain.

Scripture quotations marked (TLB) are taken from The Living Bible, copyright © 1971 by Tyndale House Foundation. Used by permission of Tyndale House Publishers, Carol Stream, Illinois 60188. All rights reserved.

Published by River Publishing
P.O. Box 292888, Tampa, FL 33687 USA

ISBN: 979-8-89342-956-5
Printed in the United States of America

FOREWORD

This book was written about the power of the vow. Taken from the 2022 Christmas and New Year's Day services that ushered in the year 2023, I teach about key times in my own life when I made a vow to God. Although this is in the context of ushering in the New Year, a vow can be made at any time of the year. There are three key components to a vow that must take place. There must be an offering made before the Lord, followed by consecration and communion. And in this book, I will lead you through these components.

Making a vow is so powerful. I can take you around the world and show you men and women that have done business with God. They have made a vow, and you can see what the Lord has done in their lives to honor that vow. And when you make a vow, you can get up every day and do only what He tells you to do, based on that vow. You'll decree, and then it happens. People will be amazed and say, "How are you doing what you are doing?" And you'll reply, "It's a place called 'a vow.'"

And what we vow is from our heart and not our head. You cannot make a vow from a place where you are comfortable in life. A vow comes from a place of discomfort and desperation. And when we make a vow, God gets in the middle of it and what was natural that you presented to Him, suddenly becomes supernatural, and you will see His Hand.

If you want to see El Shaddai, the God Who is more than enough in your life, then this is the book for you. You can make a vow and watch Him bring it to pass.

Making a vow is a holy and precious thing before the Lord. And as we enter into these end-times, and the ushering in of the King of kings and Lord of lords, this is the time to live holy, yielded, and consecrated lives to Him.

What God will do for you, history will be written about. Vows that will be made as a result of people reading this, will impact nations and the effects of which will be felt around the world. This is a prophetic message, and he who has ears to hear, let him hear what the Spirit of God is saying (Revelation 2:29). This is a time like no other to make a vow before the Lord.

1

THE VOW OF CHRISTMAS DAY

THE STATE OF THE WORLD
Everybody in the world is running around like chickens with their heads chopped off. They are trying to live longer, even people who are 80-90 years old are doing everything they can to find the "Fountain of Youth." They are looking for the cup of the "Holy Grail," so they can extend their life.

They're trying to merge with machines, to take their consciousness and put it into computers so they can live forever. You *can* live forever, but you are not going to do it without God, and you're not going to bypass God. It's impossible! You can't! "It is appointed unto men once to die, but after this the judgment" (Hebrews 9:27). You can download all your consciousness into a computer, but somebody can switch it off! There's a place in Moscow, Russia, that does cryogenics for billionaires and other people who want to have their bodies frozen. They pay huge amounts of money for their body to be cryogenically frozen and then shipped in a special capsule to Moscow. The guy running the whole place was a billionaire and he had a divorce. His wife got mad and she unplugged everything. So everybody who was frozen on ice, rotted! And it's a terrible thing but, "hell hath no fury like a woman scorned" (William Congreve).

So you can be a billionaire and think you can freeze your body and that they're going to bring you back, but you don't know that 25-40 years from now, the guy running the place will do something wrong to his wife and she'll pull the plug on you!

Man thinks he's so smart. There are people wanting to go live on Mars—it's going to be fun watching them try to do that! As for me, I'm staying right here on terra firma, on this planet, and I'm going to do what God has called me to do until the day that I'm done. And as for you reading this, you're going to do the exact same thing. You're not going anywhere. You're not going before your time, but you are going to accomplish Heaven's purpose and plan.

In this book, I want to talk to you about making a vow to do business with God, and being governed by the eternal purposes of God. I'm also going to tell you the story of our middle child, Kelly, who went home to be with the Lord on Christmas Day, 2002. I'm going to talk about the fight, and how it led to making a vow that we are now fulfilling in all we do in the ministry today. This comes from a message spoken on Christmas Day 2022, the anniversary of what took place in our life 20 years ago to the day, concerning the vow. Because at 4:37 a.m., in the early hours of Christmas morning, the room in the Intensive Care Unit at Tampa General Hospital became an altar. No one planned this, no one even talked to me about it. It was just one of those things.

HOW IT BEGAN

Our middle child, Kelly, was born with a genetic disease called cystic fibrosis and for us, each child had a one-in-four chance of having it. So after we had Kelly and Adonica was pregnant with Kenneth, the doctors wanted her to get a test to make sure he didn't have it, but we had a peace in our spirit that he was fine.

However, when Adonica was pregnant with Kelly, she knew in her heart that something was wrong. But we just kept praying over Kelly like we did over every child in the womb until the delivery. Nevertheless, when she was born, it was kind of a shock as you can imagine, when her whole stomach swelled up. With cystic fibrosis, the mucus is very, very thick so it doesn't flush out of the lungs and it clogs up everything. The first stool in the baby is like a mucous plug, called Meconium Ileus, and for Kelly, it blocked her whole stomach and caused it to swell like a soccer ball. We didn't know what was wrong with her, we just knew our baby had been born and now, her stomach was like a soccer ball.

We lived about two-and-a-half hours from the city, and we rushed down to the hospital. They looked at her and they told us it could be one of five things. They listed these five different diseases and each one was horrible. Cystic fibrosis is bad, it's a disease from hell, but it was actually the best one of what they told us. The options were horrendous.

We had to drive down to East London in the Eastern Cape, and then put her on a plane to fly down to Cape Town. My wife couldn't go with her so we went back home. I still preached that Sunday and then we packed the car and headed for Cape Town, which was probably an 10-11-hour drive.

Kelly was in the Red Cross Children's Hospital and they had to operate on her to remove the obstruction, but we didn't know how Cystic Fibrosis would affect her for the rest of her life. Basically, you have to give a child enzymes to help them digest the food because the mucus blocks everything. It messes with everything—the digestive system, the lungs, etc. And those first 18 months were really rough for us. And even the people we had around us, when they heard she had cystic fibrosis, didn't know what it was. But sometimes when people hear you're going through a situation, they want to know, "What did you do wrong to make this happen?" Like the man who was born blind and they asked, "Who sinned? This man or his parents?"—and it was neither. Stuff just happens in life. We didn't know that Adonica and I coming together could even produce anything like this. It was like walking through a door where you know you have to trust the Lord, and you have to have a peace in your heart, even though everything looks totally horrendous. We were praying for the sick all the time and laying hands on the sick, and now, we were dealing with this.

Kelly nearly died at about 11 months, and I can still remember she couldn't even keep her food down—she'd just bring it all up. My father walked through and he laid hands on her and it was instant, the thing just turned for her. It was amazing. But we knew it was a battle, it was a struggle. This thing had a hold of her lungs and it was like it had its claws in there, and the enemy just used it as a knife to just stick in us.

So every day we were dealing with it. It's not like a headache that goes away, it was there the whole time and we had to give her medication on a daily basis.

THE CRITICISM AND ATTACK

When we came to America and when the internet was birthed back in the mid-1990s, the critics went live with stuff about me on the internet. They said, "Howard-Browne doesn't believe in medicine," which was totally wrong. We did everything we could in the natural to get her healed. We got every treatment that could be used to treat her. We did whatever it took, even though I am not a fan of Big Pharma.

Today, there are certain treatments now that would have really helped her, but they have only been invented in the last 10 years. But in many ways, I'm so glad she is actually with the Lord because I can't imagine her living through the covid season, and that would have be a classic example for them, "Howard-Browne's daughter just died of covid—the pastor who wouldn't close his church. His own daughter dies of covid." My brain already saw all the headlines and all the trash they would have wanted to make up over it. You must understand, there are people who are anti-God, are anti-healing, anti-miracles, and anti-signs and wonders, so they just want to make a mockery of everything that God does. We know God heals today. Many of you reading this can say, "I've had a miracle in my lifetime." Many of us have testimonies and amazing stories of miracles that have taken place. But the critics would say we're making it up, it didn't really happen, it was psychosomatic, or it was a placebo—you just thought you were healed, but you actually weren't healed. But the fact of the matter is, it's real, it's real! Jesus still heals today.

Now a lot of ministers will never go public with a battle or a storm they faced. I'm probably one of the few ministers who actually talk about these things, but the Lord told me it would be great encouragement to share with people what took place in our life. Because you can see that if God was with me, He can be with you as well. If God can give me victory, He can give you victory as well.

We need to have a greater compassion for people who are hurting. There's a world out there that's hurting. There are people hurting every day. When you're driving down the road, people are passing by, and you have no clue if they're in an emergency, or if there's something bad that's taken place, if they've received bad news, or a bad report they've received from a doctor—people are hurting.

THE FIGHT

So the fact of the matter was that there was nothing medicine could do for her, other than just help keep her alive until the day came when she would run out of lungs, which is what took place in the early hours of Christmas morning on 25th December, 2002.

She nearly died at 18 months and at 3 years of age. And then also from the age of 3 through about 14, there were critical times every couple of years where she ended up in intensive care. And then there were times when she was fine, and you wouldn't really know what she was dealing with. She acted normally. Kelly was not one to go around and moan about being sick. She just acted like she was fine.

I still remember, in December, 2002, the whole family wanted to go skiing up in Colorado and I said to her, "Listen baby, you and me are going to stay home and the family is going to go up to Colorado. They're going to go skiing, and we'll just stay home and have fun in Florida because when you get up to high altitude, it is hard to breathe." But she said, "No Dad, I'm coming." I said, "Kelly, you're not going to be able to ski at that altitude. Even people who have normal lungs have a problem going up to that level, and it takes a day or two to get acclimatized."

If you go up into the mountains, you shouldn't exercise and exert yourself because people have died just going up into the high mountains. It's called "altitude sickness." It takes a couple of days to acclimatize and get used to it. People shouldn't just fly in and start doing rigorous stuff, they should take a couple of days to acclimatize. Kelly said, "No, absolutely not. I'm also going skiing." I said, "Kelly, you won't be able to." "No," she said, "I'm taking the oxygen tank, and I'm going to put it in my backpack and I'm skiing down that mountain!" And that was my daughter! It was hard and I couldn't talk her out of it. She said, "I'm going and there's nothing you can do about it!" I tried to bargain with her. I tried to work a deal with her and it was, "No, no, I'm going skiing. I'm putting the oxygen in my backpack and I'm skiing down the mountain."

So we went, but the moment she got up there, she couldn't really breathe. So I just stayed with her and the family skied. Then we flew back to Tampa, and I had to go preach for R.W. Schambach. Maybe some of you reading this remember that great man of God? I went to his headquarters in Tyler, Texas to preach for him. I was doing week-long meetings there, right before Christmas.

CHRISTMAS, 2002
Then my wife called me and said, "Look, they've taken her in and the doctors say this is the worst they've ever seen her." Everything had to do with lung function and oxygen, all that kind of thing. So I was praying over there, and then I flew back into Tampa. I can remember I went over to the intensive care unit in Tampa General Hospital. It was a private room, they had all the monitors up, and Kelly was sitting in the bed talking, but you could see she had a cannula and was breathing with oxygen. We were now two days out from Christmas and we were trying to get everything ready. But now we had to make changes, and we knew we were not going to be able to celebrate Christmas

as we usually did at our house. We would have to have it in the intensive care unit instead.

You can imagine trying to celebrate Christmas in intensive care when your daughter's on oxygen! They actually wanted to put her on a ventilator, but she was adamant that she wasn't going on anything. They wanted to inject her with steroids and she said, "I'm not going to let them put their steroids in me. I won't be able to have children," because she wanted to have eight children. So she was adamant about what she was, and what she wasn't going to do.

Christmas Eve, I went down to the store and I bought a diamond ring with sapphires that I wanted to give her for Christmas. And by the time I got to the hospital that evening on the 24th, she wasn't lying down in the bed, she was actually on her knees on the bed, facing the monitors and watching all the numbers on the machines. I sat down beside her, and Adonica and I were talking to her. People had come and gone. And I'll just say that I was very tired. I was running at a maximum, two meetings a day as I normally did back then. I said to my wife, "Let me go lie down for a few hours, and I'll get some sleep. Then I'll come back and you can go home, and I'll stay with her through the night."

We lived over in the New Tampa area at that time, and I went home and slept for two hours. Then I woke up, had a shower, and I felt like we were in the fight of our life. I didn't understand, and I didn't know that it would mean that Kelly was going to leave us and go home. We never planned for her death. We never talked about death. In fact, the doctors even said to us, "Have you never told your daughter she's going to die?" And we said, "No. We only told her she's going to live." And Kelly never even thought of dying. It was probably that day when I went home to go and lie down and go to sleep, that she asked the doctor for the first time, "How long do I have left?" She never even talked that way, and the doctor said, "Maybe a day, or a week."

When I arrived, I clearly remember there was a major winter storm. There was thunder and lightning, and it was starting to rain. I was driving to get to the hospital, and it was an ominous night. It was like I was driving the longest journey I had ever been on where the road never comes to an end. I got to the hospital and I said to Adonica, "Okay, Sweetie, you go and get ready for Christmas. I'll stay with her and then you join me in the morning." So Adonica went off and I was talking to Kelly. I said, "Sweetheart, I want you to have this, this is what I bought you for Christmas," and I gave her the ring. She looked at me and said, "Daddy, I'm going to be here in the morning, why are you giving this to me now? This is Christmas Eve. I'll be here in the morning." I said, "I know, but I really want you to have this now." And I gave it to her, but I could see she was distracted. When somebody's leaving the Earth, they're not really interested in something you bought them.

I know there are people who say about their loved ones, "I wish I could have bought them *this* and I wish I could have got them *that*," but if they're with the Lord and they're in Heaven, then whatever you were going to buy them or do for them was really not for them, it was for you.

LOVE ONE ANOTHER NOW

Sometimes people have regrets because they didn't do what they should have done when the person was alive. But that's why you don't want to wait till somebody gets into trouble to tell them how much you love them. And I've developed that over the years. I always just tell everybody I love them. I'll be on the phone with a heathen and I'll say, "Hey, great to talk to you. Love you, man." I just tell everybody I love them.

But we should never wait for a crisis in somebody's life to then suddenly become caring. We should be caring for one another now. We should be careful for one another and loving to one another now, not just in the bad times, but also in the good times.

In our family, we've had my daughter's funeral, my father's funeral, and my mother's funeral. At those three funerals here at the church, there were people who I only ever get to see at a funeral. They live in the central Florida area, but they never come to any meetings, they never come to one of the services, but the moment one of my family members die, they are right there. It's like, "Who are these people?" They say, "We just came just to tell you we love you." What do you mean you've come to tell me you love me? We never see you! Do you have a morbid thing with death that you only show up for funerals? Do you mind coming before the next family member dies?

I don't understand some people. Please forgive me, but I just don't understand them. They come around when the dead are there, like turkey buzzards or vultures. You never see them until there are dead people. The moment there is death, they are there. There are people in the Church who love dying and love death. That's why some churches are more like a mortuary or a funeral home. You just take one look at the ushers, and you see they are like pallbearers. You just say, "Hey, great to see you. Haven't seen you since my father died. Awesome to have you with us today!"

CROSSING INTO ETERNITY

So let me get back to Kelly's story. Now what you have to

understand is that not only was I her father, but I was her pastor, so here I was talking to my daughter and when I gave her the gift she said, "I'm going to be here tomorrow." I said, "I know, but I really would like you to have this now." So I helped her open it, put it on her hand, and she liked it. She thought it was pretty, but you could see that she was distracted because she was dealing with something else. She was dealing with stepping out of this life and crossing into eternity.

And that's something that you do by yourself. A car can go over the cliff with four people in it and they all can scream and die at the same time, but they die individually, do you understand that? When they pass, two people could go into the arms of the Lord, and the other two could go to a lost eternity. Death is something people don't really understand. The Bible says to be absent from the body is to be present with the Lord (2 Corinthians 5:8).

> IT'S NOT HOW MANY YEARS YOU LIVE, IT'S WHAT YOU DO WITH YOUR LIFE THAT COUNTS. IT'S HOW YOU MAKE YOUR LIFE COUNT FOR THE KINGDOM OF HEAVEN. IT'S WHAT YOU ARE GOING TO DO WITH YOUR LIFE TO IMPACT ETERNITY, AND WHAT YOU INVOLVE YOURSELF WITH ON A DAILY BASIS, MONDAY, TUESDAY, WEDNESDAY, THURSDAY, FRIDAY, SATURDAY, AND SUNDAY, THAT WILL COUNT 100 YEARS FROM NOW.

That's why we've got to get people saved. You don't know where these people are going. You watch people flying by on the highway. You don't know what's taking place. Listen to this testimony from England—there were soul-winners on the streets winning people to the Lord using the soul-winning script and they prayed with a certain lady. About a week later, they were back in the same area and somebody stopped them and said, "Hey, do you remember that lady that you prayed for? Remember she was argumentative with you about giving her life to Christ, but then she acquiesced and said, 'yes,' and she prayed the prayer to accept Jesus?" They continued, "You went off and got in your car and left, but that lady went around the corner and was hit by truck and was stone dead right after you prayed for her!" So that's what people don't understand, they don't see that. We *must* get people saved.

Now most people will never do what I did, and that was to be the officiator in the homegoing of my daughter. Basically, I was taking my daughter and handing her to the Lord. I didn't plan it, but that's the way that it came down.

In the ICU, Kelly said to me, "Daddy, I can't breathe," and then she said, "What are we going to do now?" What are *we* going to do now? She didn't say, "What must *I* do now?" She said, "What are *we* going to do now?" So I looked and I said, "Sweetie, if we don't get the miracle we've been believing God for over the last 18 years, then you're going to go be with Jesus." And when I said that, her whole body began to shake uncontrollably. I looked at her and said, "Kelly, are you afraid?" she said, "No, *I'm* not afraid, but *my body* is afraid." So I learned something about death in that moment—we were never created to live temporarily, we were created to live eternally, but sin came in. Then initially, people were living to 400-800 years, but God then shortened it to 120 and shortened it again to 70 or 80. Now I know there are a lot of people who want to live to 120, but I look at most people who are 100 and I think, *Let's just back it up to 70 or 80!* I'm not saying that to be mean to anybody, but even if you live to 120, when you get to Heaven, Methuselah's going to look at you and say, "Seriously? Dude, I cracked over 900 years. You could only handle 120? You're a kid! Go to kindergarten."

But it's not how many years you live, it's what you do with your life that counts. It's how you make your life count for the Kingdom of Heaven. It's what you are going to do with your life to impact eternity, and what you involve yourself with on a daily basis, Monday, Tuesday, Wednesday, Thursday, Friday Saturday, and Sunday, that will count 100 years from now.

As you are reading this, maybe there are things or issues you are worried or concerned about. But 100 years from now, you'll ask yourself the question, "What was I even concerned about? That thing was nonsense anyway. Why was I so worried about it?" Our focus must be on impacting eternity.

So I said to Kelly, "Sweetie, let's pray together right now." She said, "What are we going to pray about?" I said, "We're going to make sure that there's no unforgiveness in your heart." Of course, I knew Kelly was saved, but I just wanted to make sure that she didn't have any unforgiveness towards anybody. She said to me, "But what if I don't mean it?" I said, "Then you're going to pray it in faith. And you're going to pray this after your dad right now, and we're going to forgive everyone. Okay?"

"Yes."

"Okay. Let's pray…"

And I led her in this whole prayer, and then I saw her smile a little smile—stubborn Kelly—and she prayed the prayer and forgave everyone. Then we began to talk and I talked to her about Heaven. I got into the bed and she was on her knees in front of me. I was looking at her and as a father, everything went through my mind. I said to Kelly, "If I could take my lungs and put them in you right now and give you my lungs, and my life would end but yours would carry on, I would do that right now, but I can't. And I've prayed for you thousands of times and anybody who's anybody in the healing ministry, anywhere in the world, has prayed for you." If you name them, if they were in the healing ministries in the 1980s and the 1990s, even some of those who were holdovers from the 1960s and 1970s, they prayed for her. I found old people of 100 years old who were in the Healing Revival, and I grabbed their hand and stuck it on her head. I did everything. *And you find a lot of ministers when you have traveled to over 90 countries!*

I found a lot of preachers and people said, "This guy's a Pentecostal preacher. He had great move of God back in 1948." I'd go and talk to him, "Come here. Put your hands on my daughter." And of course, some didn't do it properly, so she had an adverse reaction to anybody coming to pray for her, which was probably detrimental. But the bottom line is, we did everything we could in the natural, and we did everything we could in the spiritual.

At this stage, Kelly couldn't breathe. She grabbed another oxygen mask and tried to hold both together over her mouth, but it was like she was drowning in the air, she couldn't breathe. I was watching my child drown right in front of me, and now I had to come up with the solution. I didn't know what I was doing. Nobody trained me to do this.

So I looked her and I said, "Hey, Sweetheart, I've got a plan." She said, "You do?" I said, "Yes. Here's what we're going to do. I'm going to pray and you're going to go to Jesus now. You're going to go to Heaven and get your new lungs, and then I'm going to call you back. I'm going to raise you from the dead. I'm going to call you back." She said, "You're going to do that?" I said, "I don't know what else to do. I've tried everything. We've had anybody you can name pray for you. I don't know what else to do." And I had a total peace. People think I must have been bawling and crying, but I was at total peace. It was like I was watching this movie—except I was in it, and I was watching this whole thing unfold in front of my eyes.

I said, "The only problem is, I don't like this idea." She said, "Why?" I said, "Because you're going to get to Heaven and then I'm going to call you back, and you are going to ignore me. I'll say, 'Kelly, come' and you'll ignore me." She said, "No, I won't, Dad." I said, "Kelly, you do now! You know that if I have to wake you up for school or something (and she just started River Bible Institute and had been in it for two or three months), you moan, 'Can I just sleep another half an hour?' And if we go to an amusement park or you're riding a roller coaster and we need to go home, you say, 'Oh, Dad, please another half an hour.' And when you get to Heaven, do you know how beautiful it is? First of all, you're going to see Jesus!"

THE REALITY OF HEAVEN

I started to describe to her what Heaven was like. I said, "You can see Him!" I was trying to put myself in her shoes as I was watching my daughter leaving the Earth. Now if anybody reading this says, "Why didn't you pray?" We had already prayed! This was not the time to pray. We'd already done that many, many times. The church had prayed. We had prayed all night. We had prayed and prayed, we'd fasted, and we had done everything. Many times, God had healed her, but what she needed was a creative miracle. So I said, "I don't like this idea because you're going to get to Heaven and then you'll ignore me. You'll hear me calling you and you'll just pretend you didn't hear your father!"

I talked about the music and I said, "You're going to hear sounds that you don't hear down here because there are not instruments here that can play the heavenly music. The colors are going to be beyond anything you've ever seen, and you're going to see Jesus. So when I call, you're going to ignore me."

And she said, "No, I won't," so I said, "Well, Kelly May Howard-Browne, do you promise your dad that if I call, you'll come?" She said, "I promise." I said, "Kelly Ma,y do you promise your father that if I call you, you'll come?" I said again, "Kelly May Howard-Browne, do you promise your father that if I call you, you'll come?" She said, "I do." I said, "Then go to Jesus now," and I took her and I pulled her right into my shoulder.

The doctors came in and I just waved them out. Down here on the Earth, there was nothing they could do, and she was not going on a ventilator. So I said to the doctors, "Just leave her. It is me, her, and Jesus." And I pulled her head in and held her, and I raised my hand and began to sing:

> *Lord, You are more precious than silver.*
> *Lord, You are more costly than gold.*
> *Lord, You are more beautiful than diamonds,*
> *And nothing I desire compares with You.*
>
> (LYNN DESHAZO)

The doctors and nurses were looking, I was singing, and she put her head on my shoulder and began to groan because she never, ever thought she was going to die. Then she went to sleep. Normally, when people run out of oxygen, they fight and have to be sedated. But the doctors didn't give her anything. She just went to sleep in my arms. My phone vibrated (which was one of those flip phones) and I pulled it out. It was my wife and I said, "Come, Kelly's going," and Adonica already knew. She was weeping at the house and she drove in. This was now probably just after 1:00 a.m. in the morning, Christmas Day, and we held her. We sang to her and really, just worshipped.

And I realized what was happening, the hospital room had become an altar, but not by choice. If you had told me three months earlier, that I would be in the intensive care unit of Tampa General Hospital worshipping the Lord, and that I would be handing my daughter to the Lord, I would have said, "Impossible. It's not going to happen." But I found myself in that place, and I had total peace.

And so we just worshiped the Lord, and at 4:37 a.m., we felt her spirit leave her body. Her body just went limp in our arms, and I knew she'd left. I said, "Goodbye, Kelly," and we just held her, and my wife and I talked. Then we got up and we talked to the doctors and nurses. Kelly left us at 4:37a.m., but I think we left the hospital about 8:00 a.m. We spent time talking to the doctors and nurses, and we headed home. Now we had to break the news to Kenneth and Kirsten, who never, ever expected this. They'd always seen a miracle—the times she went into an intensive care unit, we had always prayed and Kelly came out. But this time, we prayed and nothing happened.

I had tried everything, but you know, you can carry your children only so far. You carry them, but it's like they slip out of your grip. You're holding their hand, and then they just slip right out of your grip. That's what it felt like. And it was as if she and the Lord had something going on that I couldn't interfere in.

THE LOVE FROM THE BODY OF CHRIST
So we got home and told Kenneth and Kirsten. As you can

imagine, nobody was going to have Christmas that day. The presents were there, but we didn't even look at them. Everything changed. And then the phone started ringing. The calls were coming in from ministers, people I knew, some I didn't know, and even some major ministries who I thought would never even talk to me, called me out of the blue and just said, "We want you to know, we love you and we are praying for you." It was the most shocking thing to me. I had *never* felt so much love from the Body of Christ. Because remember, we had come through the revival of the 1990s, and we had a decade of being slammed every which way but loose! We were attacked for the joy and now ministers were calling us to say, "We just want you to know we love you and we're praying for you." I thought, *Wow! There are people who actually do love us!*

I had not known that because I had never felt that before. All I ever heard was the criticism and the attack. The phone rang for days. If I name the names who called, you'd know them. All of the greats, many of whom have now gone home to be with the Lord, called me, prayed with me, and talked to me. And I said to them, "Well, it's not over yet because I told Kelly that I'm going to call her back." There were one or two top healing ministries who said, "Don't do it. It's not a good idea to do that," but I just felt I had to do it. It wasn't something I was going to do for days and days, I'd set a cut-off day.

Obviously, we couldn't bury her that Christmas week. We had to wait till the next week, but I wanted to bury her before we went into 2003. I wanted to get everything done between Christmas and New Year. Then we could start the New Year with that behind us. Everything was about a new beginning.

We had to hold off on the funeral because that Christmas Eve, there had been so many deaths in Tampa due to the storm.

So it was a deadly night. They said, "Look, you can only do the funeral on Tuesday," so I said, "Get the body delivered to the church on Monday, and I'm going to pray the whole day. I'll start in the morning at 9:00 a.m., and I'll go till 5:00 p.m. If she's not back, then we'll just send her back to the funeral home and commit her body to the ground the next day. But I said I was going to pray, so I'm going to pray. Because I'm not going to get to Heaven and have Kelly look at me and say, 'Hello, Dad. You chickened out. You said you'd call and you didn't.' But I'll get to Heaven and tap her on the shoulder and say, 'I told you, you wouldn't come back!'"

I preached that Sunday morning and night at the church. In fact, the title of my message that morning was, "Let's have a resurrection." There were so many people praying. We received calls from all over from people saying, "We are praying, Pastor. This is not done yet." And I could go on and tell you all about the people who called us.

THE OVERWHELMING PEACE OF GOD
Monday morning, we had the body delivered and they brought it upstairs. They couldn't get the coffin up, so they carried her out of the coffin and put her on a bed in my office. Pastors Eric and Jennifer were praying and many other staff members were all praying. Many people were praying, but they didn't know we had brought the body up to the ministry.

I went in and laid down next to her on the bed, and I put my hand on her body. She had been dead now several days. The body had come out of refrigeration. She was still wearing the same outfit she wore when she died. I put my hand on her and you could feel ice, but as I put my hand on her, a peace hit me that is beyond anything you could ever even begin to describe.

As I put my hand on her, I was thinking to myself, *This is crazy! This is the body of my daughter, but I have just peace in my life.* It was as if I was immediately in Heaven. Such total peace! I didn't cry, I wasn't weeping or sad.

Obviously we loved Kelly, we didn't want her to be gone. She would have been 40 years of age this year (2024), and somebody we really would have needed. (Now I don't know how some people would have got on with her, because she was very direct! She had a little bit of me and some of her mother in her, a combination of Adonica and myself.) But as I put my hand on her on Earth, the peace of God flooded my life and I heard the voice of the Lord say to me, "She's run her race." I didn't say anything verbally out loud, but in myself I said, "What do You mean, 'She's run her race'? She's only 18!" (I talk to the Lord like that!) The Lord said to me, "Some people's races are longer than others." I said, "Okay." I never mentioned it to my wife or to Kirsten who was there, or anybody. I just said, "We're going to pray till 5:00 p.m."

But now, how do you pray for somebody to be raised from the dead? Do you want to know how you pray for somebody to be raised from the dead? If this ever happens to you, I'll tell you how to bring them back. Someone says, "Yes, but you didn't bring her back." No, but I've talked to people who have raised several people from the dead and they asked me, "What did you do?" And when I told them what I did and they said, "If she was coming back, then she would have come back to that." And in January 2023, during the Winter Campmeeting, our head of security dropped dead in the middle of the service, and I did the very thing I'm about to tell you. Although he was dead for some minutes, he came back to life and is back at work with us today. It is very simple to raise the dead, and this is what that you do:

"Father, in the Name of Jesus, I rebuke the spirit of death. And I command life." (But you don't just say it passively. You have to take authority over it.) "I take authority over death. And I speak life!" And you pray, "Life! Life! In the Name of Jesus, life! I speak life!"

So if you want to pray religious prayers, you won't want to be around me, especially if you are going to raise the dead. And let me just say that if you pray in a weak voice, "Lord, if you could please bring our daughter back to us? Amen," that's not even a prayer!

THE TRANCE

So we prayed, "Life," the whole day until about 4:30 p.m. I would come and go, my wife prayed and other people prayed. At about 4:30 in the afternoon, the anointing was so strong in that place. It was like you could feel the whole building move, and then suddenly, it was gone. You could feel anointing, but then, it was as if it was gone, and I knew it was over. I said to my wife, "It's time. I'm letting her go now." I didn't know that Pastor Eric was in prayer in the next room, and he actually went into a trance. He only told us this the next day when we went to commit her body to the ground for burial. He said, "Pastor, you know at 4:30 yesterday afternoon, I was in a trance. I left my body and I went to Heaven." I said, "You did? What did you do?" He said, "I went to Heaven and I was looking for Kelly, and I found her." I said, "You found Kelly?" He said, "Yes." I said, "What was she doing?" He said, "She was on her knees, she had her hands raised, and she was worshipping God."

And he said, "But it was like everything around it was blurred and the Lord wouldn't let me see anything else, but I saw Kelly. And I said to her, 'Kelly, Kelly, come.'" And she turned and she looked at Pastor Eric and the first thing out of her mouth was, "What are you doing here?" Which is just like my daughter! It was as if she was saying, "Who let you in here?" And Pastor Eric told me he said to her, "Your dad's calling. He's calling from the Earth. Come, it's time to go." And when he said that, two lights appeared that came from the throne and one went down to the Earth. And when it went down, he and Kelly looked from Heaven, and they were right above the roof of the church, and could see her body. The light went down onto her chest area and Pastor Eric could see me praying. The light was right where she was and this was about 4:30 p.m. when the anointing was the most intense. The other light went to the throne, which Pastor Eric said he knew was an angel. Pastor Eric said to Kelly, "Look, they are getting your new lungs!" and he said that Kelly looked down and when she saw her body, she pulled a face and said, "Oh, yuck! I hate that thing."

Her reaction to seeing her physical body was one of total disgust. Just as if you had been eating something that was distasteful and you spat it out of your mouth, and then people wanted to bring it back to you on a plate for you to eat. That body was the thing she was confined to for 18 years. That body was the thing that restricted her. That body was the thing that stopped her from singing—which is what she did all the time from when she was a little baby. She always wanted to sing, that was her dream. And now Pastor Eric was telling her, "Come, you're getting new lungs. Come, you're going to go back into that body." But she looked down and said, "Oh, yuck! I hate that thing!"

And let me ask you a question as you are reading this. If you were up in glory in Heaven, in the presence of God, and people were trying to get you back into your physical body, would you want to come back? Whether you had anything wrong with your body or not, would you want to come back? I can promise you right now, there's no way I'd come back. I'd say, "Hey, I'm done with that. It is over!"

So Pastor Eric said, "No, Kelly, come. It's time to go. Your dad's calling you right now," and then she looked and she said, "No, the way it works is, you go first. You go first." And of course, he said he then came around, back in the office. But when he told me that, it really was a peace to me because I knew that she'd heard me. And if you could have heard the way I prayed, I promise you the whole of Heaven heard me!

We had an individual who was working for the ministry at the time, who later on became an administrator with us. He was trying to come up the elevator that afternoon, and he said he thought the whole building moved. He said, "Man, I don't know what they're doing in there, but this whole building shifted." We were doing business with God.

THE VOW

Now if I go back to the early hours of the morning, I was holding my daughter in my arms just after 1:00 a.m. and she was against my chest. I was singing, "Lord, you are more precious than silver," and I was making a vow. I was making a Christmas Day vow to the Lord. I was making a vow to the Lord and also telling the devil, "This is going to cost you big time. You made a wrong move here by touching my daughter today." And I said to the Lord, "Today, I give You my best gift. I worship You with my best gift. I know You didn't ask for her. I lay her down, and I give You the best that I have. If I live another 50 years, I couldn't give more. A billion dollars would be like two cents —it would be nothing. Today, I give You my best gift.

I worship You with my best gift on this, Your birthday. But I make a vow today, that the devil will pay. I vow 100 million souls and $1 billion into world missions. That's my vow."

> KELLY WAS MY FIGHT. THAT'S WHY I BOOKED ALL THOSE MEETINGS. THAT'S WHY I BOOKED MEETINGS BACK TO BACK, BECAUSE SHE BEGAN TO BE ATTACKED. SO I'D TELL THE DEVIL, "THAT'LL COST YOU," AND I'D A BOOK A MEETING.

As of this writing, we're sitting now on nearly 47 million decisions. It's happening! It is happening! It is taking place.

The next day, we committed her body to the ground for the Day of Resurrection, and the Lord supernaturally sustained us over those last couple of days of December, and then all through January, February, and March. It was really Easter 2003, when there was an Easter conference here at The River, when for whatever reason, it hit us! We were sustained January, February, and March. Then Easter it hit, and we couldn't even come out of the house.

I don't weep much about it now, but Christmas Day morning 2022, it hit me hard because in the service, we saw all the pictures of her when she was a baby, and of course, you miss the person. It's not something you're going to get over, because you miss that person. It wasn't a suddenly, it wasn't something that happened out of the ordinary. It was a battle. It was a fight for 18 long years.

Kelly was my fight. That's why I booked all those meetings. That's why I booked meetings back to back, because she began to be attacked. So I'd tell the devil, "That'll cost you," and I'd a book a meeting. "I'm going to Alaska, I'm going to preach here. I'm going to the Arctic. I'm going to preach in the frozen wasteland. I'm going to get penguins saved. I'm going to the Outback. I'm going everywhere." And now that she's gone home, we are going after the 100 million souls and the $1 billion into world missions. So either way, the devil's lost majorly.

But I share this today because I really want this to be an encouragement to people who have gone through stuff. Maybe you haven't lost a child, but you've had setbacks. And I know exactly where she is, so we didn't really "lose her" as she's with the Lord. And even if she said to me, "Daddy, I can come back now," I'd say, "Kelly, don't, it's all fine. We've got it sewn up. You just keep rejoicing over there. I'll see you, we'll be there with you and it's not going to be long. So you just carry on up there, and I'm busy working hard down here to bring in the harvest of souls to what I made a vow to." Because unless the Lord gave you a special assignment, why would you want to come back? What would be the reason?

PUTTING EVERYTHING ON THE ALTAR

Now I'm saying this too because some people say, "Well, I don't really want to live anyway, so I'd like my life to come to an end." Why would you want to end your life if you've never come to a place where you've surrendered your life?

Why would you want your life to end? You might say, "Well, I'm just tired of life as it is?" Yes, life can get tiring without God, without His power, and without His anointing. But you have nothing to lose, so why don't you put your whole life on the altar and say to the Lord, "Today, I give You my whole life. If You'll take the remainder of my life and use me, then I'll do whatever You want me to do. Regardless of what I've been through, regardless of the storms that have come my way, regardless of the attacks that have come against my life, I make a vow that my remaining days, whether I've got 5 years or 50 years left, I promise You, these remaining days of my life will be used for You and Your Kingdom. And they're not going to be used for the enemy. I'm not going to play two worlds. I'm not going to live with one foot in the Kingdom and one foot out of the Kingdom."

We've had people come to The River who have been on the brink of suicide and God totally flipped their whole life around. And now, the Lord is using them in a powerful way. So if you are reading this and you are feeling like you just want to end your life, I come against that! I come against the spirit of suicide. I come against the thought of ending your life. Today, your life will begin anew and afresh. So place your life in the hands of the Lord.

What I'm sharing with you now is important and I am holding nothing back. There are many more details about Kelly that we could get into, but it is what it is. I don't hold anything against God at all. We are totally happy. "As for God, his way is perfect" (Psalm 18:30).

MAKE THE DEVIL PAY FOR WHAT HE'S DONE
It is about being governed by the eternal purposes of God. You might say, "Yes, but I'd like to live my life." Not only will you live your life, you'll enjoy your life and God will bless you with everything else that other people want. And God will give it to you and bless you, if you'll serve Him with every fiber of your being. Make the devil pay for what he's done to you, your family, and your loved ones. Make the enemy pay—this is going to cost him! It is going to be very costly for him. It's going to cost him in souls.

That's why even the business you get involved in, it's not to make money so you can survive. The last thing on your mind is survival, "I just need to pay the bills." The last thing you should be thinking is paying the bills. You're making money to fund the end-time harvest and embarking on the greatest adventure of your life that 100 years from today will still speak. The new churches that will be planted and funded; the missionaries that will be sent to far-flung corners of the globe; the people who will be raised up—they will all speak! Why do you think we scholarship everybody here at River University? Do you think I'm stupid? Show me another university that scholarships everybody!

Somebody says, "Do you have a scholarship fund?" There is no scholarship fund—we pray it in. Everything we do here is different. The way we run things and how we function, it's all different. But I know this for a fact, "Except the Lord build the house, they labour in vain that build it: except the Lord keep the city, the watchman waketh but in vain" (Psalm 127:1).

> IT IS ABOUT BEING GOVERNED BY THE ETERNAL PURPOSES OF GOD.

DO BUSINESS WITH GOD

So I want you to pray about the vow. I can't push you into a vow. This is something you have to get real about with God. But it would be great for you to make a fresh vow to God concerning your life, and especially for the next three years. Do business with God. "They that go down to the sea in ships, that do business in great waters; these see the works of the Lord, and his wonders in the deep" (Psalm 107:23-24).

An intensive care unit in a general hospital is deep waters. It's a storm like you couldn't even be prepared for. And I'm not sharing this with you for you to feel sorry for me. I'm actually sharing this with you so you can help me bring in the harvest of souls. Somebody says, "How do I help?" Well, you didn't have a daughter die in your arms on Christmas Day, but you've had other things happen. So instead of allowing those things to set you back, attach the setbacks to a vow and win souls.

Otherwise, you don't even want to carry on, and you'll get mad at God, at the church, and at the preachers. You'll say, "I'm never going back. I was around those ministries. My God. They preach healing, but my own child died. My dog died. My parakeet died. My goldfish died." And you'll blame God, when God has done nothing but only been good! All He's been is good!

The Lord said to me, "Do you trust Me with your life?" God wants you to come to that place where you trust Him with your life.

> YOU DIDN'T HAVE A DAUGHTER DIE IN YOUR ARMS ON CHRISTMAS DAY, BUT YOU'VE HAD OTHER THINGS HAPPEN. SO INSTEAD OF ALLOWING THOSE THINGS TO SET YOU BACK, ATTACH THE SETBACKS TO A VOW AND WIN SOULS.

LOCK YOURSELF INTO THE WILL OF GOD

If you're a young person reading this today, you're not going to miss out on one thing. You're going to be blessed beyond measure. If you're an older person reading this today, there won't be any regrets concerning your life, because God's going to take the remaining days of your life and make them count for eternity. God can take the next three years and make them equivalent to 40 or 50 years. There won't be any regrets.

This is why we're doing what we do at The River. That's

why The Stand is going on. I tell The River Church, there's no "quit" button on me. I don't have a tap-out button. I might be unconscious, but I'm not tapping out. I'm just telling you right now, it ain't going to happen!

And you have to lock yourself into the will of God. And all I can tell you is that He's good. Where have you heard preachers saying, "My daughter died in my arms, but I want you to know the Lord is good?" But I can tell you, "He's a good God. He's a great God. He is a mighty God!"

Each year, I play the recording of Kelly singing "Silent Night" (Franz Xaver [music], Joseph Mohr [words]). When I see her face on the screen, I see my face in hers! I actually recorded the film myself with a handheld camera in an empty auditorium. I said to Kelly, "When you finish this, look down at me and smile," and that's on the film. I didn't realize that this would be put together after she went home to be with the Lord. She's watching from Heaven and she's hearing the souls that are coming in, because the Bible says all of Heaven rejoices over one sinner who comes to repentance (Luke 15:7). So for every sinner who comes to repentance as a result of this ministry, the noise is being heard in Heaven and Kelly is saying, "My dad's working again. He's fulfilling what he said he would do."

Then I play the recording of her singing, "The Perfect Tree" (Ray Boltz). This was filmed in the parking lot of the church with my car doors open and with the song playing through the sound system. Later on, we put the music on and I love that. I wish I had recorded more of these moments. She actually could never sing a whole song because she'd sing a line or two and start to cough. So when we recorded the album, it was the first time we really heard her sing. We said, "Wow! You've got to be kidding me!" But she can sing now for sure!

KELLY'S VISION

Below is something that Kelly wrote whilst at Bible School. It's her vision of what she felt called to do. She actually wrote it for me as the assignment from her first year class because I walked into the class and said, "Okay, students. I want you to write for me on both sides of a piece of paper, what you feel you are called to do." They gave her paper to me probably six to eight weeks after she went home to the Lord, and when I read it I thought, *Are you kidding me?*

So this is the River Bible Institute assignment dated October 16th, 2002, by Kelly Howard-Browne, student ID number 1694, for Dr. Rodney Howard-Browne:

I feel called to world evangelism, revival, and a music ministry. I want to travel anywhere God takes me, and sing, preach, and teach. I want to travel to other nations where you need an interpreter, but I want to be able to speak in English (without an interpreter) and the people will understand me, because the Holy Spirit will translate my (His) words to them. (This might only be necessary when I'm not able to find a translator, but still, it would be awesome.) Also, I want to be translated from place to place—every once in a while or whatever. (That would also be awesome.) I want to travel to the deep jungles of Africa, Spain, Asia, India, Europe, and the Middle East, as well as wherever God wants me to go. Also Russia, probably the Ukraine, Norway, Greece, and Rome.

I feel compelled to everywhere I go, to raise up a church with a school, a Bible school, a hospital (where we'll attract the unsaved with the Word "Hospital" and we will pray for them and get them saved and healed), an orphanage and a food and clothing ministry.

> *Once I go to a place and get a lot of people saved, I'll train them to flow in revival and win souls and run the whole ministry there. Then, I'll move on to the next place and to souls, have revival, and establish a local place where the work of God can continue, then I'll move on to the next place and so on. God is Awesome!!*

She wanted the supernatural! And of course, I don't know where she got the ideas from for stuff like this! But when I read it, I thought to myself, *Lord, give me a break. She can't even do that.* And do you know, the Lord always laughs at me? I heard Him laugh and say, "Oh, really?" I said, "What do you mean?" He said, "What do you think she's going to do during the millennial reign? For 1,000 years, she'll be translated from place to place, she'll speak in the language of the people without needing an interpreter." So she was actually describing what she will be doing during the millennial reign of Christ. So everybody can look and think it's all over, but it's not over. There's *nothing* over for the believer.

KELLY'S SONG

This is also a song she wrote which one day we will put music to:

> *I look through my window, at Your face*
> *Giv'n me love and peace and Your grace*
> *With Your strength I live on, in this wide place.*
> *My peace sustained in You*
>
> <u>Chorus</u>
> *All that I do, I do for You.*
> *I exalt You above all else*
> *And when I see your face, it melts my heart*

THE VOW

Your power so penetrates
Giv'n all I have trained for all my life.
I will serve You always in mind, in my heart, and my soul
To You, I freely give
To You freely give

Thank You Lord for Jesus Christ
For the Holy Spirit that brings the light
We're able to spread revival through this land

FULFILLING THE VOW

So I pray this has been an encouragement to you, and that you have heard the Lord speak to you about your own life. Make the devil pay! There are some things you can change, and there are some things you've just got to roll with. And if I had to do it all over again, I would choose the same path. I would still want Kelly in my life, because Kelly made me who and what I am today. She was my fight.

If you saw the criticism we took from her death. The critics made a website and the headline of the website said, "Is he still laughing now?" Because Kelly had died. And still over 20 years later I can say, "Yes! We're still laughing, Bro! Still laughing," because God is still on our side. Thank You, Lord Jesus.

So everything we are doing around the ministry is to fulfill the vow. It's not about building a big ministry. To be honest, I don't really care too much about that. I've been around many ministries and I hear all the talk. I know what to do and what not to do. With everything we do, we only want to do it if God wants us to. We're not looking to outshine anybody. We're not in competition with anybody. We're not trying to beat anybody or anyone. We have one enemy, and we know who he is.

We will help any person who wants to win souls and give their life to the Lord for God's eternal purpose. We will help them and we will go out of our way. We'll spend our resources and do everything we can to help each person accomplish Heaven's purpose and plan for their life. That's why this ministry is here. That's why are we here. And that's why we're here with The Stand.

JACOB'S VOW

Turn to Genesis 28:10–22, "And Jacob went out from Beer-sheba, and went toward Haran. And he lighted upon a certain place, and tarried there all night, because the sun was set; and he took of the stones of that place, and put them for his pillows, and lay down in that place to sleep." (vv. 10-11). I don't know if you have ever slept outside on the ground, but a stone is not a pillow. Have you ever had to sleep on the ground? You can dig a hole for your hip, but it never works.

"And he dreamed, and behold a ladder set up on the earth, and the top of it reached to heaven: and behold the angels of God ascending and descending on it" (v. 12). So Jacob came to this place where there was a heavenly interaction between his life and Almighty God, much like what happened to me over 20 years ago in that hospital room.

> And, behold, the LORD stood above it, and said, I am the LORD God of Abraham thy father, and the God of Isaac: the land whereon thou liest, to thee will I give it, and to thy seed; and thy seed shall be as the dust of the earth, and thou shalt spread abroad to the west, and to the east, and to the north, and to the south: and in thee and in thy seed shall all the families of the earth be blessed. And, behold,

THE VOW

> I am with thee, and will keep thee in all places whither thou goest, and will bring thee again into this land; for I will not leave thee, until I have done that which I have spoken to thee of. And Jacob awaked out of his sleep, and he said, Surely the LORD is in this place; and I knew it not.
>
> (VV. 13-16)

HAVING A DIVINE INTERSECTION

So there will be times in your life when there will be what I call a divine intersection between you and God, and it doesn't have to happen or take place in the church. In fact, for most people, it'll never happen in church because their church is not even conducive for that. We endeavor to create that place here at The Stand and at Revival Ministries International, where people can have that divine intersection and have an encounter with God. That's what our whole ministry is about. We know when Heaven interacts with you, something takes place. You and God do business, and then supernatural things are going to be made manifest.

As I can tell you already, just in the 27 years of the River Church and the 26 years of River University, there are thousands who have gone out of here, and there are miracles taking place through their life, because of a divine intersection, where they had what I would call, a head-on collision with the Holy Ghost.

So all I do is arrange the "accident!" I know what I'm doing. I arrange the "accident" on purpose! People come here to The River and they don't even know what's going to happen. And then suddenly, God grabs ahold of their life, and it's over, it's over!

And, behold, I am with thee, and will keep thee in

all places whither thou goest, and will bring thee again into this land; for I will not leave thee, until I have done that which I have spoken to thee of. And Jacob awaked out of his sleep, and he said, Surely the LORD is in this place; and I knew it not. And he was afraid, and said, How dreadful is this place! this is none other but the house of God, and this is the gate of heaven. And Jacob rose up early in the morning, and took the stone that he had put for his pillows, and set it up for a pillar, and poured oil upon the top of it. And he called the name of that place Bethel: but the name of that city was called Luz at the first.

(VV. 15-19)

So here, Jacob is erecting an altar in that hard place. One of the things interesting to note here is that God already told him everything He was going to do. Jacob then goes on to make a vow, but God already told him what He was going to do. God said, "I'm going to bring you to this place. I'm going to give you all of this."

GOD INITIATES THE VOW

THE VOW LOCKS YOU IN.

So in his vow, all that Jacob was doing was reiterating back to God what God had already said to him. Jacob wasn't initiating anything God hadn't initiated to begin with. Jacob wasn't coming up with it.

Likewise, I was always on a quest for the harvest of souls but then I vowed, "One hundred million souls." I was always on a quest for the harvest of souls and I believed that God was going to allow us to fund the end-time harvest. I didn't know how that would happen, but in that moment of that divine intersection, was the time of the vow. People will criticize you and say all kinds of things about you, but they weren't there. You can say what you like about Jacob, but you weren't there. You didn't have the dream. You weren't the one who heard God say those things and then came back at God with what He had already said. Because God said, "Put Me in remembrance of My Word" (see Isaiah 43:26).

So God speaks to you, and then you remind Him of what He told you. And it sounds like you're the one coming up with the idea, but really, it's not you. He's already said that for you. He's already spoken that over your life, you are just coming back at Him with what He's already said to you. "Well, I made a vow to God." But the Lord's saying, "You're not doing anything I didn't already promise you." But the thing with the vow is, it locks you in.

So Jacob vowed a vow. Now he's repeating to God everything God already said to him, but he says, "If God will be with me, and will keep me in this way that I go, and will give me bread to eat, and raiment to put on, so that I come again to my father's house in peace; then shall the Lord be my God" (vv. 20-21). God already said, "I'm going to be that for you." Verse 22 continues:

> And this stone, which I have set for a pillar, shall be God's house: and of all that thou shalt give me I will surely give the tenth unto thee.

Now I personally would like to tell the Lord, "Everything

You give me, I'll give You 90 percent." Because even the tenth He gives you will be so big, you won't even have a place to put it!

MAKING YOUR VOW

I want you to pray about this and actually write some things down that are personalized to you. You can use the form at the back of this book and then at the conclusion of the book, we are going to pray over these things.

I want you to make a list, writing down what God has spoken to you over these last three years. And then be in prayer, laying it before God in a vow to say, "Lord, this is what I want to talk to You about." And do that covering the next three years.

The fire of God is falling. If you need a touch, a special touch, just reach out. He'll come and touch you right where you are. Thank You, Lord. Special anointings are being poured out. Just reach out and receive what Heaven has. Thank You, Lord Jesus. We worship You. Wonderful Jesus!

SURRENDER YOUR LIFE TODAY

And if you are reading this and you don't know Jesus as your Lord and Savior, pray this after me and just invite Him into your life:

> *Father, I come to You. I surrender my life to You today. Even as the story has come forth of Pastor, who gave his daughter to You on Christmas Day, I give myself to You, and I receive You as my Lord and Savior. Forgive me of my sin. Wash me in Your Blood. Thank You for dying for me on the cross. And from this day, I'm going to serve You all the days of my life. And I thank You for that even now. In Jesus' Name.*

If you prayed that prayer, find a church that preaches the

full Gospel, that lives in the Book of Acts and the power of the Holy Ghost, and believes that Jesus is coming very soon. Then get busy starting to win souls. Because the only thing you can take with you when you leave the Earth is people. Amen.

2

EARLIER VOWS

THE UPCOMING YEARS
What the Lord is about to do in these upcoming years, is going to overshadow everything we are seeing right now. These next years are going to be even more over-the-top. The Lord is so good. I believe it was Abraham Lincoln who said people are about as happy as they decide to be. Because you can look at life through a negative lens and see everything bad, and it will become like a self-fulfilling prophecy, or you can look at the good. It's the same as, "is the glass half full or half empty?" But it's not just us wishing, hoping, or keep making something up, it's about God's Word.

It's about keeping our eyes on His Word and appropriating His Word and His blessings in our life. And it's so important at this time for every church in America to stand strong, be bold, and preach the Gospel, not being ashamed, not making excuses, and not bending over backwards for ungodly people.

We don't do what the ungodly people think we should do. We do what the Word tells us to do, what Jesus tells us to do and what the Holy Ghost tells us to do. So for you who are reading this, I pray boldness on you to really get a revelation of how much God has done for you, how much Jesus has done for you, and that all the blessings and promises are yours, and you can stand up and appropriate them.

You see a lot of social media where people are mockers. Before social media, you didn't have to listen to them (and you don't have to listen to them now), but people are always posting stuff mocking the Word. And even some people claiming to be Christians are mocking miracles and mocking tongues. But this is the time when we stand out and even more pray in tongues, cast out devils, lay hands on the sick, and get people saved, healed, and delivered.

These upcoming years, we refuse to be poor. We refuse to beg. We refuse to struggle, and we decide we will be blessed. We will be blessed and we will be a blessing. King David said this, and I claim it for myself and I pray it over everybody reading this, "You are blessed, and you are a blessing." Say it over yourself, "I am blessed, and I am a blessing."

> I AM BLESSED, AND I AM A BLESSING.

I read an article recently that said Tampa is the best city in Florida. It's the best city to live in, and I don't think that's a coincidence. I believe that's because The River Church is here, and we're making a difference in the city. The stats they look at cover the way the city is laid out, including all the museums, the public transportation, etc., and the crime. But the crime rate is low because we go out on the streets and we preach Jesus! We go outside the walls and tell people about Jesus and bring them in. And we're going to keep doing that! Hallelujah!

And more than ever before, we have got to give the young people a purpose. We must give young people something to live for, something to look forward to, and something to believe in. There are many things we are believing God for, for these upcoming years, but I think even more so, we're going to believe to touch this younger generation, because they're hungry for something that's real. And every devil in hell is going after them, but we're going to snatch them out of the gates of hell.

I just feel such an excitement for these upcoming years, and I can't wait to see what the Lord is going to do. We look forward to the goodness of God, the blessing of God, and that He's going to use each and every one of us to do great and mighty things, in Jesus' Name. Amen.

> THE WHOLE WORLD IS LOOKING FOR CHANGE, BUT THAT CHANGE IS NOT AN EVENT. THAT CHANGE IS A PERSON, AND HIS NAME IS JESUS.

But let me just get a few things out of the way here regarding the future. If you're not serving the Lord, it's going to be very bad for you. It's not going to get better, it's going to be hell on Earth for those who don't want to serve God. Someone says, "Pastor, be nice." I'd like to be, but I'm telling you it's going to be the worst thing you've ever seen. These upcoming years will be proof that people have lost their minds permanently, starting in Washington, D.C., in the Congress and the Senate, and in every place in between.

But God is laughing at them. They thought they would stop the Church, but when you touch the Church, you touch the apple of His eye, and He will not allow you to do that. So while they have an agenda of a One-World Government, one money system and the rise of the Antichrist, God is ripping to shreds every one of their plans and purposes. Because this is not the hour of the Antichrist. This is the hour of the Body of Christ to accomplish Heaven's purpose and plan. Therefore, the Lord is not with them. He's with us and because He's with us, they will fail. Everything they're planning for us will fail!

You'll see wars and rumors of wars, famine, drought, plague, sickness and disease, poverty, lack, death, and destruction on every side. But God's people will be in the cleft of the Rock, hidden in the secret place of the Most High, and abiding under the shadow of the Almighty (see Psalm 91:1). And you will see the Hand of God in an accelerated way.

Do you know that the recent number one worldwide question Google was asked was, "Can I change my life?" People are stuck in a dead-end street wanting to change their life. The whole world is looking for change, but that change is not an event. That change is a person, and His Name is Jesus.

These upcoming years will be the greatest years of harvest the Body of Christ has ever seen globally. If you are a minister of the Gospel, an evangelist, or a missionary, your ministry will see such an acceleration of the harvest of souls, the likes of which will make every other year look pale in comparison to what is coming, because of the hunger that is out there in the world. People are looking for someone, they think it's a person, but they don't know it's Jesus. And if you bring Jesus to them, it's going to be a complete turnaround, and it's going to be miraculous as never seen before.

It is what was prophesied of old and even said by many greats, of what would happen before the return of the King. We are it, ladies and gentlemen, and we're going to usher in the return of the King of kings and the Lord of lords.

The release of the financial overflow shall take place over these next few years. And I'm not talking about what's dependent on somebody else, I'm talking about what you have in your hand. You and God are a majority, and what He has put in your hand, and what you've been faithful to hold in your hand, shall now be multiplied, and you shall see it take place.

This "occupying until He comes" (see Luke 19:13) shall be more evident than before. Just like you come on this property at The River Church and you can see what God's doing for the church, it shall be that way for your personal life and even for your home and everything you touch. Friends, family, and people who know you will come around you and they'll shake their heads and say, "Please, can you tell us what are you doing? We've known you for many years and we don't understand. What happened to you?" And you will just look at them and smile and say, "It's the Hand of God. It's the Hand of the Lord that is caused this to happen."

And the Body of Christ that will not compromise, will take more territory than has ever been taken in history, from the Book of Acts until now. And what I'm talking about will be made manifest in the natural realm. I'm talking about land, buildings, and properties. I'm talking about things that will shock individuals and you'll see it happen. Churches will be built, and new churches will spring up. Bible schools will be established, and we will see the Gospel go out as never before. Don't listen to the lies of Barna, the reviews, and the nut-job polls that say the Church is declining. Yes, the dead religious church is declining, but the Church of Jesus Christ is not declining, it's on the increase. Hallelujah!

And new ministries will be launched. There are things you're doing right now, but there will be new things God will have you do. You'll do innovative things, things that are cutting edge and things that will reach groups of people who up to this point, have never been reached before. And you're going to see it happen. It is going to be supernatural. Many will even try to come and fathom out what's happening and say, "We don't even understand it. How did you do this?" And you'll say, "Well, the Lord spoke to me in a dream. God spoke to me to do this, I just stepped out." They'll say, "How much money did you have to do it?" And you'll say, "I had nothing other than the Word of the Lord, and I got up and went about my daily business and everything has accelerated."

If you take the example of Operation Eden here at Revival Ministries International (R.M.I.) Headquarters, at the beginning of one year, it was just bush. But within that year, look what happened with all the food being produced—it's going to be like that. I'm talking about acceleration. Because that's how it's been for us walking around here at R.M.I. Our jaws have dropped open! This is a time like no other to make a vow.

THE POWER OF THE VOW

> A VOW ALWAYS COMES OUT OF A PLACE OF DISCOMFORT, AND OF EMERGENCY. BECAUSE WHEN YOU COME TO THE PLACE OF A VOW, IT IS AS IF YOU ARE NEGOTIATING WITH GOD.

I want to talk to you about the *power* of the vow and I feel led of the Lord to run through some key times in my own life where I made a vow to God. Now God holds a vow as something that is holy. No one can make a vow for you. Only *you* can make a vow in your heart.

And a vow never comes out of a place of being comfortable. A vow always comes out of a place of discomfort, and of emergency. Because when you come to the place of a vow, it is as if you are negotiating with God. You realize, *I'm in trouble. I need some help, and I need divine help. I need divine intervention. Without divine intervention, I'm not going to make it.*

As you know, we are living in perilous times and those who will be totally yielded and submitted to the Spirit of God, will be carried by the Lord. Because many stand on the brink of each New Year saying, "What about the New Year? What does the future hold? Will it bring good things? Will it bring bad things?" All I know is that for those who serve God, and whose lives are 100% sold out to Him, there might be some storms you'll go through and some unexpected things that come out of the blue, but God by His Hand, shall deliver you, and it shall be *speedily* (see Psalm 31:2)!

Now I'm not talking about something you get yourself into by your own stupidity. Obviously, we've told you how to get out of those situations—you cry, "Help!" to the Lord! So I'm not talking to people who are going to go out and do something dumb. I'm talking to wise people who are going to make wise decisions, based on the Word of God, and what God's plan is for their lives.

"For I know the plans I have for you, says the Lord. They are plans for good and not for evil, to give you a future and a hope" (Jeremiah 29:11 TLB). These are the plans He has for you. So whilst I can see the handwriting on the wall for whole nations that stand on the brink of total economic collapse and the finances of the planet are set to implode, it's just smoke and mirrors at this point, because I know God *will* sustain His people!

EL-SHADDAI—THE GOD WHO IS MORE THAN ENOUGH

> EVERY YEAR IS THE YEAR OF EL-SHADDAI, BUT YOU'LL KNOW IT THESE UPCOMING YEARS, AND YOU'LL EXPERIENCE IT FOR YOURSELF.

As I was praying about these upcoming years, what I felt in my spirit was so big. There were many things I wrote down, but everything I wrote down was not sufficient to describe what I felt.

But I heard this in my spirit loud and clear—that there's no other way to describe these upcoming years than to let you know that it shall be "El Shaddai!"—The God Who is more than enough!

Previously, I've talked about the double and the double portion, but I can tell you that for the next years, there's not even anything we can measure it by! I'm not saying it'll be three times or four times, because that is insignificant to what I feel in my spirit! Hallelujah!

And what you've even seen happening with the building here at The River Church since August, 2022, likewise, things will happen in four to six months that normally would take five years to do. The acceleration shall be so great. It's got nothing to do with double, triple, or quadruple — it is El-Shaddai, the God Who is more than enough!

You will see it in your personal life. You will see it in your home. You will see it in your marriage. You will see it in your children. You will see it in your grandchildren. You will see it in your great-grandchildren. You will see it in your business. You will see it in your ministry. You will see it in your walk. You will see it in your talk, and every day when you get up out of bed. From sunrise to sunset you'll say, "Wow!" And it's not going to be something you will sit and try to make happen. It is something that He does.

Every year is the year of El-Shaddai, yes, but you'll know it these upcoming years, and you'll experience it for yourself.

You'll say, "I've seen that happen for other people, I never thought it was going to happen for me, but something is happening." You'll ask your wife, or your husband, "Is this even real? Pinch me! Is this even happening?"

MAKING A VOW

God's speaking to you about everything He's going to do for you as you are reading this. You can either receive the Word of the Lord now, or you can receive the word of the devil!

Turn again to Genesis 28:10–22 and we will look at this vow in more detail:

> And Jacob went out from Beersheba, and went toward Haran. And he lighted upon a certain place, and tarried there all night, because the sun was set; and he took of the stones of that place, and put them for his pillows, and lay down in that place to sleep.
>
> (VV. 10-11)

I've often thought about this because I've slept outside on the grass. I've slept outside in the bush, and I went to Australia and slept in the Outback on the ground with a fire next to me.

Kangaroos were jumping around me. I know the ground is not very comfortable. You can't really move a rock around like you do a pillow. You can flip a pillow whichever way. You don't wake up and there's a rock with a big dent in it. Jacob used a rock as his pillow and personally, I don't know if I would ever choose a rock to be my pillow. Whenever I've read this I've thought, *Man, it looks like he was between a rock and a hard place!*

But while he lay asleep,

> ... he dreamed, and behold a ladder set up on the earth, and the top of it reached to heaven: and behold the angels of God ascending and descending on it. And, behold, the Lord stood above it, and said, I am the Lord God of Abraham thy father, and the God of Isaac: the land whereon thou liest, to thee will I give it, and to thy seed.
>
> (VV. 12-13)

What I've also realized is that there is a fight against the believer for any property. The devil does not want you to have land or property. But God says that the upcoming years shall be the years of your land and your property. Hallelujah!

> And thy seed shall be as the dust of the earth, and thou shalt spread abroad to the west, and to the east, and to the north, and to the south: and in thee and in thy seed shall all the families of the earth be blessed.
>
> (V. 14)

Now you have to understand that Jacob wasn't praying. He just was tired and went to sleep, and God talked to him in a dream. And there are people reading this with dreams on the inside of you. You just think you had a dream, but you don't realize, God actually spoke to you in a dream. Maybe you didn't identify it when the Lord was speaking to you, but that dream, nonetheless, is still a dream on the inside of you.

God said, "And, behold, I am with thee, and will keep thee in all places whither thou goest, and will bring thee again into this land; for I will not leave thee, until I have done that which I have spoken to thee of" (v. 15).

So this is not Jacob asking God for one thing. This is Jacob having a dream and God telling Jacob everything He is going to do for him. Somebody says, "Yes, but the Lord hasn't spoken to me about everything He is going to do for me." God's speaking to you about everything He's going to do for you as you are reading this. You can either receive the Word of the Lord now, or you can receive the word of the devil—which you can do by watching CNN or mainstream media!

"And Jacob awaked out of his sleep, and he said, Surely the Lord is in this place; and I knew it not" (v. 16). Jacob was afraid. Why? Because when God comes to you in that way, it shakes you to the very core. That's what happened to me in the early hours of March 17, 2020, when a fire came in my room at ten minutes past two o'clock in the morning. It shook me to the core. I still tremble and quake when I think about that night.

"And he was afraid, and said, How dreadful is this place! this is none other but the house of God, and this is the gate of heaven" (v. 17). Now the word "dreadful," basically could be used as meaning, "awe," "overwhelming," or "life-shaking," because you cannot meet the Creator of Heaven and Earth and just be normal after that. And this was none other than the gate of Heaven.

THE VOW

> And Jacob rose up early in the morning, and took the stone that he had put for his pillows, and set it up for a pillar, and poured oil upon the top of it. And he called the name of that place Bethel: but the name of that city was called Luz at the first. And Jacob vowed a vow, saying, If God will be with me, and will keep me in this way that I go, and will give me bread to eat, and raiment to put on, So that I come again to my father's house in peace; then shall the LORD be my God: and this stone, which I have set for a pillar, shall be God's house: and of all that thou shalt give me I will surely give the tenth unto thee.
>
> (VV. 18-22)

FIRST THE OIL AND THEN THE VOW

So the place where Jacob slept, the place of the dream, now became an altar. Then Jacob poured oil upon it and he's doing something that he wasn't even told to do. It was something initiated out of his own heart. In other words, he had this dream and then he felt, *I need to make a vow*—which is what I'm going to challenge you to do. Obviously, I can't force you to do this. It's something *you* witness with and feel in *your* spirit.

Somebody may say, "Pastor, I've done several of these." That's fine. This is a new hour. Each year, each day is going into a time that no one's ever lived in before, but the Holy Ghost has already been through the upcoming years and the future beyond. The Holy Ghost has been through January, February, March, April, May, June, July, August, September, October, November, and December. The Holy Ghost has been through the following year. And the Holy Ghost has been through the year after that. And He Who has already probed into those years, already knows what is to come. And He Who knows what is to come, shall lead and guide His people by His Spirit, so you'll move through everything the enemy throws in your path. And nothing the enemy has planned shall ever set you back. Every time the enemy tries to attack you, you'll come out stronger, greater, and better than before.

So Jacob made this altar, and he poured oil upon it. He called the name of this place, "Bethel," and now, Jacob makes a vow. God never said to him, "If you make a vow, then I will do this and that." Years ago, I read this and I thought, *Look, I'm not an idiot. My mother did not raise a dummy. If they did that in Bible days, I'm going to do the same thing.* Because I've been through many hard places. I've found myself crying, "Help!" I have found myself just in a hard place, where I got up every day and did what I normally do, but I found myself in a situation where I needed God's divine Hand.

With over 42 years of marriage, at the turn of each year, Adonica and I pray together, consecrate our lives afresh, and make another vow to the Lord. And we look back over the past year and say, "Okay, whatever was of the flesh, please let it be removed from us. However many weeks out of the 52 weeks we were in the wrong direction, please forgive us. Let this upcoming year be a year that we don't miss the mark in any way and that we don't spin our wheels." We're making tracks. We're moving forward. We're doing exactly what God has called us to do.

So Jacob just does this of his own free will. And one thing I know about the Lord is that He will never force anything on you. He only responds to how you respond to Him. In other words, Jacob had a dream and then he came up with this vow of his own free will.

There are dreams on the inside of every single one of you reading this, but you must come of your own free will and say, "Okay, if the Lord will do what He said He would do, if God will do this, this and this, then I vow of what I feel in my spirit…" and make your vow. Because there are things I feel in my spirit that I've been talking to the Lord about for a long time. There are things we've been waiting 15 years for that are about to be made manifest, that will bless this ministry *and* the Body of Christ worldwide.

"So Jacob vowed a vow saying if God will be with me and will keep me in the way that I go" (see v. 20). God had already said, "I'm going to be with you" (see v. 15). If I was God I would ask, "What are you talking about? I already said I'd be with you. I already said I'm going to keep you. What are you talking about?" But what Jacob was doing was responding to the Word of the Lord, "Okay, if this is what God said, and He will do what He said He will do, then I'm going to do this." What do you mean? Well, it's not a one-sided thing at that juncture, it's double-sided. God's going to do this, and I'm going to do that. We know what God's going to do these next years, but what are *you* going to do?

> GOD ONLY RESPONDS TO HOW YOU RESPOND TO HIM.

Genesis 28:20, "If you keep me in the way that I go and give me bread to eat" (which He will), "give me raiment, clothes to put on" (to where you'll have so many clothes you'll have to give half of them away because you can't wear them all). "And this stone, which I have set for a pillar, shall be God's house: and of all that thou shalt give me I will surely give the tenth unto thee" (v. 22). When you think about it, God didn't even ask him for any of that. *Jacob's* the one who's coming up with that. This is so holy.

A YEAR OF DECREEING

> IT IS VERY IMPORTANT THAT YOU SEPARATE YOURSELF FROM ANYTHING THAT IS INVOLVING INIQUITY IN ANY WAY, SHAPE, OR FASHION.

Now, go with me to the Book of Job. And I know when I mention Job, people say, "Oh no. Can any good thing come from Job?" Yes! Let's go to Job 22:23.

> If thou return to the Almighty, thou shalt be built up, thou shalt put away iniquity far from thy tabernacles.

It is very important that you separate yourself from anything that is involving iniquity in any way, shape, or fashion.

> Then shalt thou lay up gold as dust, and the gold of Ophir as the stones of the brooks.
>
> (V. 24)

Now you can look at this two ways: that it is just dirt, or that you have so much of it that is just like dirt. Gold will be just like dirt because it means nothing to you. People will say, "Oh look at all this, it's just piled up like dirt." This was the case for Solomon where they had silver dumps outside the city. Imagine, silver dumps! So much silver that someone says, "Where are you going?"

"I'm going to the dump."

"What are you going to do there?"

"We have so much silver, we just dump it outside the city!"

Job 22:25 continues, "Yea, the Almighty shall be thy defence, and thou shalt have plenty of silver." That's why you don't have to worry. Obviously, we tell people to protect themselves and be wise, but the Almighty will be your defense.

Therefore, you will never fear, or be afraid. No matter where you go—by land, by sea, or by air. You'll be able to walk in the war-torn territories. You'll be able to walk into the middle of where hell is breaking loose, and you won't even fear a thing. For the Lord your God is your defense. And no one will snuff your life out before its time. Even if they fire bullets at you, the bullets will fall to the ground at their feet, because the Hand of God shall sustain you.

The Almighty will be your defense and you'll have plenty of silver. You'll have so much gold, it'll be like dust, you'll have plenty of silver. Why? Because the silver is His, and the gold is His (see Haggai 2:8).

Now I know when you start talking along these lines, people immediately say, "Oh, I had better go and buy gold and silver." No, it will come *to you*, it will come *into your hands*.

> For then shalt thou have thy delight in the Almighty, and shalt lift up thy face unto God. Thou shalt make thy prayer unto him, and he shall hear thee, and thou shalt pay thy vows. Thou shalt also decree a thing, and it shall be established unto thee: and the light shall shine upon thy ways.
>
> (VV. 26-28)

You'll decree it! What does that mean? Well, you'll be going along and a situation may arise that sounds like bad news. It sounds like things are going awry, but you'll say, "No!" And you'll decree, and it turns out differently from what the plan was. So you live a life of declarations—the devil's not going to have your family, he's not going to have your children, he's not going to have your grandchildren, he's not going to have your great-grandchildren. He's not going to have your family members. Your family is not going to go to hell because today, you set the tone. Today, you set the tone for the upcoming years and for your life. I feel the anointing of the Holy Ghost so strong here.

> LIVE A LIFE OF DECLARATIONS.

THE FIRST MAJOR VOW

> HEAVEN IS BEYOND ANYTHING YOU CAN EVER IMAGINE. THERE ARE NOT ENOUGH WORDS IN THE ENGLISH LANGUAGE TO DESCRIBE THE GLORIES OF THE REALM TO COME, AND WHAT'S ACTUALLY WAITING FOR YOU. THAT'S WHY NOTHING THE ENEMY HAS HERE ON THE EARTH IS WORTH TAKING TO GIVE UP WHAT GOD HAS FOR YOU IN ETERNITY.

Previously, I spoke about the vow of Christmas Day, and I'll refer to that briefly again later. But this was not the first time I made a vow to the Lord. I was born-again at the age of five, baptized in the Holy Spirit when I was eight, and there have been many times over the years I've prayed and talked to the Lord.

I talked to Him when I was at school, I spoke to Him about things that I was dealing with and made what I call, "mini vows," which at the time were major to me. Looking back now, they were mini, but the Lord gets you ready. You make a lot of little vows en route to the big ones, and all of them are important.

But I would say that the most life-changing moment for me came in August 1978. My family was very close. I have two older brothers—one who was 14 years older than me, and one who is 12 years older. My brother who is 12 years older than me is still alive, and he's in the ministry today. God uses him in a powerful way.

My eldest brother, when he was 31 years of age, died suddenly of leukemia. We didn't realize what had taken place because he was washing his hands in a chemical called carbon tetrachloride which went straight into his bloodstream. Within six months, he was dead.

And that's something that just rocks your whole world. It was the last thing we ever even thought about. You never go through your life thinking your oldest brother's going to die. He was in the ministry and we had a band. He taught me to play guitar and we sang together. He was starting to do crusades and then suddenly, he was dead. It was crazy. They came and fetched me from school and said, "Your brother just passed." I said, "What?" We rushed to the house, shocked. My second oldest brother lived, probably a five-hour journey away, and he drove up. He looked at me and I said, "What are we going to do?" We were out in the country and they didn't want to come pick up the body until the next day, so we had the body lying in a bed there for basically a day. My older brother said, "We're going to pray, and we're going to raise him from the dead right now," I said, "We're going to do that?" He said, "Yes." I was

17, he was 29, and we started to pray. I'll never forget that—it was life-changing just being there.

And the Lord spoke to both myself and my brother and basically said, "I want to bring him back, but he doesn't want to come back. He doesn't want to come back." Now somebody says, "Well, the Lord can make him come back." I think when you get on the other side, if the Lord says to you, "You know you should go back." You'd say, "Please, if You don't mind, can I just stay here? I don't really want to go back." Because people don't realize how wonderful Heaven is.

Heaven is beyond anything you can ever imagine. There are not enough words in the English language to describe the glories of the realm to come and what's actually waiting for you. That's why nothing the enemy has here on the Earth is worth taking to give up what God has for you in eternity

I could go into the whole thing of praying for hours, but I'll leave it at that. My brother's corpse was there, and I had my hand on him and we were calling, "Life, in Jesus' Name!" But we realized, my brother did not want to come back.

Somebody says, "Well, you really have had great success raising the dead!" Well, at least we do it! At least we do pray. How many dead have you prayed for? I've prayed for many dead—there's a couple of dead people reading this now I'm praying for! But I can remember standing there over the corpse, and this is what I said to the devil, "You will rue the day that you touched my family. Today, I make a vow." And I didn't know what I was saying. No one told me to make these words up, they just came out of my mouth. I said, "You will regret this day and you will pay for what you've done to my family. This is going to cost you greatly." And here's what I said next, "People are going to laugh at you around the world. They're going to laugh at you!"

THE VOW

I did not know God would give us a ministry of joy that would carry us to over 90 countries of the world thus far. So what does that mean? If you make a vow, do you think God will let those vows come to nothing? Absolutely not! If your heart is pure, you mean business with God, and you make a vow, it shall come to pass according to that which you have vowed. And I know some people might not believe any of this stuff, but then this book is not for you, so go and read something else!

People say, "Well, God is sovereign." Yes, God is sovereign. You'll find yourself in the middle of what Sovereign God is doing, and you'll cry out from your innermost being and God sovereignly by His Hand will come and intervene in your life, and you will see the Hand of God. I could take you around the world right now, and I'll show you men and women who have done business with God. I'll show you men and women for whom the Hand of God is all they'll ever see.

What God will do for you, history will be written about. Vows that will be made today by God's people as a result of reading this, history will be written about. This is Holy Ground. I vowed people all over the world will laugh at the devil. I had no idea God would give us a ministry of joy—which would be equally mocked.

But it doesn't matter who you are, or where you're from. Just because you make a vow and God begins to bring it to pass, doesn't mean to say you're going to get a free run up the side. The enemy will still try to come against you and do whatever he can. So you must keep your eyes and focus only on Him.

> WHAT GOD WILL DO FOR YOU, HISTORY WILL BE WRITTEN ABOUT. VOWS THAT WILL BE MADE TODAY BY GOD'S PEOPLE AS A RESULT OF READING THIS, HISTORY WILL BE WRITTEN ABOUT.

THE SECOND MAJOR VOW

So that was in 1978, and in 1979, the Lord touched me with His fire. And in the first ten years, Adonica hooked her chariot, her caboose, up to mine, and what a glorious day that was. Then let me fast-forward because the Lord reminded me of another time in 1985 that I made a vow. I was part of a large ministry at that time and one of the senior professors at a Bible school of 550 students. I taught twice a day, morning and evening, and that's how the Lord really taught me about everything that needs to be done for a Bible school. I was one of the pastors there, but the persecution at the Bible school was so great. People mocked me openly, and I'm talking about the other teachers!

I'd get into the classroom and preach, and the power of God would fall. Then afterwards, the other teachers would mockingly say, "Did you get them all saved? Did they all get healed?" Bodies would be flying everywhere and other teachers got jealous. And I wasn't even trying to do anything! I'd just get up and the power of God would fall. I can't stop the power of God from falling. It is what it is. You know if you turn me loose on the microphone, there is going to be trouble. I'm not looking for trouble but it's just going to happen. There's going to be trouble for the devil. The power of God begins to fall, God begins to touch people, and people get healed, delivered, and set free. And people get jealous over that.

I can still remember one of the men who actually ran the whole place, was mocking me. I was probably only about 24 or 25 years old at the time. I walked in his office and I didn't mean to do this, but I grabbed him by the scruff of his neck and shoved him against the wall. I looked at him and said, "Let me tell you, you can go back to doing what you were doing before you even accepted the call to the ministry, I have nothing else *but* the call of God. Now back off!" I didn't hurt him, but it was one of those "moments." And there might be some of those "moments" where you know you can't back down. Somebody says, "Well, Jesus wouldn't have done that." Well, I'm not Jesus. I wish I was more like Him, but I'm not. I'm a work in progress, so don't pick on me on the wrong day and then get upset because something went wrong. You got "ministered" to by the fivefold ministry and the laying on of hands, and I slapped the tar out of you!

> IF YOUR HEART IS PURE, YOU MEAN BUSINESS WITH GOD, AND YOU MAKE A VOW, IT SHALL COME TO PASS ACCORDING TO THAT WHICH YOU HAVE VOWED.

I taught in the mornings and evenings and that left the afternoons free, and I went home. We lived right on the golf course, so I went to play golf. One time, I was by myself pulling my golf cart along, and I was so grieved by the persecution. I was so grieved by being attacked every day just for preaching the Gospel in an environment where there shouldn't be any adversity. It should have been a place where you should be a family together. Everybody should love the anointing of the power of Heaven and the Word of God. Why would there be opposition? Why would there be jealousy? And I can remember actually walking down the fairway weeping, and I said to the Lord, "What You called me to from a boy and what You put inside of me, I'm under major persecution for right now. But I promise You, if You get me out of this mess, if You take me out of this place and You carry me around the world, I will give You all the glory, praise, and honor. And I will take what You place on the inside of me, and I will give it away to as many people as possible."

Well, at the end of 1987, we moved to America. In 1989, revival broke out, and it picked up through 1991 and 1992. In 1993, it exploded and in 1994, it went around the world. In 1995, I was back in southern Africa. I had one day and I said, "I want to go and play golf." I never remembered what had happened before, I just went to play golf on the course I used to live on. (They actually play the South African Open on this course even now—it's a great course.) I went there and I'm telling you, the Lord swatted me. I was going along and I could see the little apartment that Adonica and I lived in. I could see where we lived and where we moved. I remembered how we struggled even to make the payments, how by the third of the month, everything we had was gone, but we gritted our teeth and said, "Bless God, we're going to serve God and we'll go over the top with God." I came to the hole and teed off. As I was walking along, the Lord took me back ten years. I saw where God had brought us from and where He had taken us to and the Lord said, "You thought I'd forgotten. I heard you on this fairway. I heard you when you cried out. Son, look what I have done." And I couldn't even play. I was a wreck. I was weeping. I said, "Lord, You've done it." You see, God is looking for what we say we will do, if He fulfills His part. That's all He's looking for.

God can cause the next three years to be like 30 years in your life. So don't take this day lightly!

THE THIRD MAJOR VOW
So then if we jump to December 25th, 2002, there I was in the Tampa General Hospital, holding my daughter in my arms and she was dying. Nobody prepared me for that moment. I found

myself saying again, "You're going to pay, you're going to pay. It's going to cost you dearly. Today, I give the Lord my best gift. I worship Him with my best gift on this Christmas Day, but I make a vow of 100 million souls (and we just crossed 46 million souls as of October 2023) and $1 billion into world missions. And I'm going to put 1,000 young ladies into the full-time ministry."

Well, with all the Bible schools, with over 10,000 people graduated worldwide, there are many young ladies who are out there and you'll hear of them in the days to come, and of what God's doing in and through their lives.

> THE BEST IS YET TO COME. I'M TELLING YOU RIGHT NOW, THIS IS THE GREATEST MOMENT TO BE ALIVE IN THE HISTORY OF THE PLANET! AND GOD HAS HAND-PICKED EVERY SINGLE ONE OF YOU TO BE HERE TODAY AND AT THIS MOMENT.

I can remember driving down the road from my house, which is an hour away from The River Church, and I was worshipping God with music playing, and the Lord spoke to me and said, "I brought the first vow to pass"—in other words, people laughing at the devil all over the world—"and I'll bring the second one to pass as well." And I couldn't even drive. I had to pull over the side of the road. I would have been arrested for DUI because I was under the anointing of the Holy Ghost. So I know how holy this is.

And you might think I'm crazy. You might think I've lost my mind, but I have not. I'm totally sane. I'm not normal, but I'm totally sane and of a sound mind. "I, Rodney Howard-Browne write this, that I am of a sound mind. And I do declare to you today that God, Who brought the first vow to pass, will bring the next to pass." And what you don't realize is that this vow is involving every single one of you reading this. This is not something that I will do by myself. This is something that God, using us all, will do. Together we will mobilize the multitudes and the people of God to accomplish the purpose of Heaven. Because there will be people *you* can reach that I can never reach. There will be places *you* will go, that I can never go. There will be doors that open to *you*, that will not be open for me.

That's why we don't desire what another person has. The grace upon you to run that race might not be upon another, but everyone reading this today, running the race with the grace that's upon you, will accomplish Heaven's purpose and plan. And great and mighty things shall be accomplished, for the best is yet to come. I'm telling you right now, this is the greatest moment to be alive in the history of the planet! And God has hand-picked every single one of you to be here today and at this moment. You are hand-picked by God, and 100 years from today, if Jesus tarries, most of us will be on the other side watching from the banisters of Heaven. And we will be looking at each other and saying, "Yes, it was our hour. It was our moment." Men and women reading this today will even change the future of America. What the enemy had planned, will be set back. The devil will say, "Oh, hell! They're doing it. They are stopping me and I can't accomplish what I wanted to accomplish. I'm going to have to wait for this generation to be evacuated out. I'm not going to be able to do what I thought I was going to do, because there's a group of men and women who will not compromise or bow their knee. They have a single purpose with a single mind, and they are focused." Oh, hallelujah!

Some of you reading this don't even realize it, but you're about to find out in the upcoming years. You're about to find out. You are going to be sitting and suddenly, it'll be like a light bulb going on, and you'll realize, "Oh, my God! Oh, that's me! That's me! That's me! Hallelujah!"

Wherever you are right now, this is for you. I speak by the Spirit of God. This is a prophetic message. He who has ears to hear, let him hear what the Spirit of God is saying (see Revelation 2:17).

Somebody says, "Are you talking to me personally?" I'm speaking to every one of you *personally*. You can either let it go by you to someone else, or you can say, "It's mine, and I'm receiving this word of the Lord today." And you'll find out that some of the setbacks you've had were actually catapults, to launch you into what God has for your life. It shall come to pass. It *shall* come to pass.

I'm just going to pause and let that marinate in you for a while. You have to see what I'm talking about in the overall plan of Heaven, because we are raising up people to go to the far-flung corners of the globe. We are raising up ministers, apostles, prophets, evangelists, pastors, and teachers. Not everyone will stand in those offices, but everyone will stand in the place that God has for them. And when you stand in the fullness of what God has for you, it will enhance everything He's doing.

But it won't be that one person is greater than the other. But rather, we will all work together to accomplish Heaven's purpose and plan. And even those for whom it looks like what they're doing is behind the scenes, Heaven sees. For to accomplish the work, everyone must take their place, and there's a place for everyone. So don't let the enemy lie to you and say that just because you don't have a pulpit, or you're not doing *this* or *that*, or you are not doing it like somebody else is doing it, that it doesn't count. It's what God has for you, not what God has for somebody else. It's what God has for *you*—that place that He has for *you*. When I look around this ministry, and I see the team the Lord has put together, I know there's no way we could do what we do without this entire team. Everybody is a part of what God is doing.

I don't know what your altar is because I'm not facing what you're facing. I don't know what you are believing God for. I'm here to stir you up, to spur you on, and to point the way. Look at what God's doing with this African boy, who was probably the most unlikely. So much so, that when we came to America and everything exploded, it made all the ministers here angry and question, "How did he get in?" Everywhere we went, people said, "Who let this kid in the door? He didn't come through the ranks. He didn't come through the denomination. He didn't come through this group, he didn't come through that group, how in the world did he get in?" Because they want you to come through a certain realm. But let me tell you, when God has His Hand on you, God will raise you up from obscurity. And when God assigns something to your life, there's no devil in hell that can stop you from accomplishing Heaven's purpose and plan. You have to understand that today.

> WHEN GOD HAS HIS HAND ON YOU, GOD WILL RAISE YOU UP FROM OBSCURITY. AND WHEN GOD ASSIGNS SOMETHING TO YOUR LIFE, THERE'S NO DEVIL IN HELL THAT CAN STOP YOU FROM ACCOMPLISHING HEAVEN'S PURPOSE AND PLAN.

THE PLACE CALLED, "A VOW"

Recently, I was talking to my wife and I said, "Sweetheart, what an adventure this has been!" And I think maybe sometimes she thinks I planned it, but I never did. I told her, "I haven't planned anything. I just got up every day and did what came my way. And that's how we find ourselves in this thing. When you married me, you didn't know you would be embarking on an adventure, where we never really knew what was going to happen. But we knew anything can happen, and probably will!"

And I know there are a lot of people who look at me and think I plan and strategize for hours. I don't do any of that. I do absolutely none of it. I don't live my life planning and strategizing. I live my life and let God "cook" what He's cooking on the inside, and I just get up every day and do *only* what He tells me to do. And then when I feel that anointing, based on the vow, I decree, and then it pops and it happens. And people say, "How are you doing it?" It's a place called, "A Vow."

And I'll be making many more vows between now and the time Jesus comes to take me home. Somebody says, "What are you going to do when you get to the 100 million souls?" We will go for 200 million at that juncture. We are not going to stop. Hallelujah!

Today is a day where we pour oil. So write down things you are believing God for and seal it between now and completing this book (see page 89).

What we vow is from our heart, not our head. Somebody says, "I think I'll vow to..." No, you don't *think* anything. It's something that comes right out of your heart, and only you can do. A lot of people want us to vow for them, "Can you make the vow for me?" No! What happens today is between you and God, so you can look back and say to yourself, "At this specific time and date, sitting and reading this book, I felt challenged of God to make a vow. And I made a vow, and look what the Lord has done!"

There are three parts to making a vow and this is the first part—making a sacrificial offering:

1. A SACRIFICIAL OFFERING

> WHEN SOMEONE DOES BUSINESS WITH GOD, THE DEVIL'S THE ONE WHO WILL BE SAYING, "IT'S REALLY ROUGH!"

We pour our oil, we bring our gifts, and we bring our worship. We bring that which has been made sacred and holy by way of a sacrifice. Somebody says, "You mean it's going to involve an offering?" You can choose today to pour your oil and bring your gift to the Lord, giving an offering. Or you can just read this book and put it down again without making an offering. Because I've met bucket plunkers and regular church attendees, and nothing supernatural happens for them. The only thing that comes at them is bugs on a windshield and that's all they ever have—another day of bugs on a windshield! You meet them and they have bugs stuck in their teeth, and a big welt mark from a bug on their head. It's all they ever have. You ask, "How's it going?" They say, "Really rough." But when someone does business with God, the devil's the one who will be saying, "It's really rough!"

Many people usher in the New Year under the influence of alcohol, hoping that somehow, the next New Year is going to be different. They are under the influence of alcohol, boozing themselves into oblivion by midnight. They're slurring their speeches, they'll find themselves with some strange woman of the night—a snaggletooth they picked up—wondering why their life is a worse hell in this coming year, than it was last year.

Because they were in the wrong place at the wrong time. It's not funny—it's terrible to be lost. It's horrendous to be lost and on your way to hell, with no hope. You can have all the money in the world, but have no hope and lost without God. And maybe as you are reading this, you are wondering why your life hasn't changed, why it is worse this year than last year.

But at The River, you are in the company of the redeemed, the Blood-bought ones, those who have been purchased with His Blood. You don't belong to yourself, you belong to Him. I don't belong to myself, I belong to Him. I am His purchase. I'm not here to do my own bidding, I'm here to do *His* bidding. It's not what I want, it's what does *He* want? It's not my will, but *His* will. It's where you lay your life down and say, "Everything I have, and everything I am, is Yours."

Someone says, "Well that doesn't look like a deal." Let me tell you, that's all God asks for. Then God gets in the middle and even that which you present to Him in the natural, suddenly becomes supernatural, and you'll begin to see His Hand. Hallelujah!

And for some person who was just "ordinary," suddenly a coal comes off the altar and is placed on their mouth, and when they speak, they speak not as a man speaks, but they speak as an oracle of God. Jeremiah 23:29 says, "Is not my word like as a fire? saith the Lord; and like a hammer that breaketh the rock in pieces?"

What will come out of River University shall not be little muppet heads or little Instagram one liners, hashtag *this*, hashtag *that*. No! When you speak, men and women will shake and tremble under the Word of the Lord, because you are not a parrot, but you shall echo Him. You will speak the Word of the Lord and it will echo through you. He will speak, and it will be echoed through you. I'm so tired of dead social media posts with no anointing! Gag me with a spoon. That is not going to shake the world!

Today is a day of great business with God, and this business is related to your future. Whatever you did before now was from the past and it's been dealt with. Today is now. Glory to God.

So take the opportunity to sow seed, and then I'm going to lead you through consecration and into communion. Those of you who mean business with God are not ready for what's about to happen. You're not ready! Because all God's looking for is a yielded vessel, that's all! It's not what *you* do, it's what *He's* going to do through you. And what He does through you, He doesn't do overnight. What He does through you has to be walked out.

There are many of you reading this who have known Jehovah-Jireh, which is a place where the Lord met you. But these upcoming years, you'll know the Person. You'll move from a place to the Person, and you'll move to El Shaddai, the God Who is more than enough. And I prophesy over every single one of you reading this, you will never, ever lack. You will *never* lack!

> ALL GOD'S LOOKING FOR IS A YIELDED VESSEL, THAT'S ALL! IT'S NOT WHAT YOU DO, IT'S WHAT HE'S GOING TO DO THROUGH YOU. AND WHAT HE DOES THROUGH YOU, HE DOESN'T DO OVERNIGHT. WHAT HE DOES THROUGH YOU HAS TO BE WALKED OUT.

A VOW COMES FROM A PLACE OF DISCOMFORT

Everything God does with you will be much bigger than what you're dealing with now. So I'm just going to tell you, do not make a vow if you are comfortable with your life right now, and you're happy with it being that way. Because you're going to step into a realm that you've never walked in before.

When God tells you, "I'm going to give you that mountain," He's not going to settle for some molehill. And it's time to take these mountains. Someone says, "Pastor, it is bigger than anything I can ever imagine." Yes, exactly, that's why you'd better be consecrated. That's why you'd better grab ahold of what I'm talking about here. Big things! Somebody says, "There he goes again about the big things." Well, I'm so sorry. I can't help it because we have a BIG God. A *mighty* God! I walk around The River and I just shake my head because I know none of this was planned. Everything was just day by day,

"Do this."

"Okay."

"Do this."

"Okay."

And that's how it shall be with you.

So before the prayer of consecration, take the opportunity to sow and be a part of what we are doing here at Revival Ministries International (R.M.I). I'm not begging, it is just totally between you and the Lord. God will speak to you and you must be obedient.

> IT'S THE SEED THAT INITIATES THE MIRACLE OF WHAT YOU ARE BELIEVING GOD FOR.

Obey the Holy Ghost in your vow to Him. You set the tone for your future even by your offering today. So just close your eyes and ask God what He would have you do. Be a part of what God's doing. This is Holy Ground. Someone says, "What am I doing?" You're pouring oil. You cannot buy what I'm talking about, it's free. But you can be a part of the 100 million souls and what God is doing here at The River.

I'm going to pray over you:

Father, even as You speak to the hearts of Your people about sowing, just as You've taken Adonica and I through this many, many years. As we made a vow to You, and brought of our seed, our treasure, we worship You. I pray for increase and multiplication on every side. I pray even by Your Mighty Hand that Lord, You come and have Your way with Your people today. Not only those here at The River, but all those who are reading this book. I speak supernatural breakthroughs on every side, even as people take what's precious to them and pour it on the altar today, that You will meet them. And then, Lord, after that, as we go to praying over the lists that they have made, with the many prayers and supplications that they've made unto You, that Lord, You hear, You honor, and You cause it to come to pass. That the next 12 months shall be the greatest of months they've ever had.

Regardless of what happens in the world, even in a time of great upheaval and the shaking of the nations, Your people shall be firm and strong. They will not be shaken, but shall endure. And we thank You for it.

And Father, we just thank You even as people make a vow today, not just verbally, and not just over these things that they've written down, but as they sow a seed today—something that's tangible, that they've put into the ministry, that they are sanctifying and setting it apart. This represents souls that will come into the Kingdom. That this offering today signifies what they are believing You for in the upcoming years. Let this offering be significant today. Let this be a time to remember as the moment they crossed over into another dimension. And we thank You for it, and give You praise, honor, and glory. In Jesus' Name. Amen.

This is holy. I have many people who contact me and they remind me of a certain time and place, where they made a vow just like you are doing today, and they tell me all the Lord has done. And let me just say this, I know there are people who have needs. All of that means nothing. Somebody says, "Well, I need some major breakthroughs this month." Listen, your breakthrough is based on what's happening here right now. This catapults you into your breakthrough. When you look at what you have in your hand and say, "This can't bring the miracle." No, but it's the seed that initiates the miracle of what you are believing God for. And for everybody it's different. I can remember when we first stepped out with a couple of hundred dollars, and that made us shake. And then when God told us to do $1,000, Lord have mercy, that was the end. But then God tells you to do more and more. But it's all His anyway!

There are things God has prepared for you that are only in your deepest desires and dreams. And when you're walking with Him and watching the Lord fulfill them to the point where there is no natural explanation for it, all you'll say is, "Wow!" There is no natural explanation to it.

For this ministry, look what happened just since the first week of August 2022, where the auditorium was gutted within a matter of ten days, and then look what the Lord has done since then! In December 2022, I declared, "And you watch what's going to happen in the next 22 days of 2023. In three weeks, that whole area will be transformed into a sanctuary. All of the sound, lights, drywalls, ceilings, paint, wallpaper, carpets, chairs, and everything! This place will be like a beehive. It has been since August 2022, but shall be even more. And the teams will be working around the clock as they have been." I showed up at all hours of the night during this time. I showed up here at 1:00 a.m. one morning and there were people working at the sanctuary. Somebody says, "Pastor, why did you just show up?" I came to watch what the Lord was doing. They never knew when they were going to see me. I just showed right up. Security never knew when I was there and by the time security found me, I had already been through the place three times. I'm teasing, but I just walked around just looking at what the Lord was doing.

And of course, you can now see the finished sanctuary today, which was completed in five-and-a-half months, and was ready for the Winter Campmeeting 2023, just as I declared!

And that's also what you're going to do—you'll just be watching what the Lord does. There are young people and children reading this, and you're going to watch what the Lord does. There are some children reading this who are going to see breakthroughs for their family. There are young people reading this who are going to see breakthroughs on behalf of their family because their parents are really not with it, but God will bypass them and do it through the young people. And the parents' jaws will drop open and they'll say, "I think I'd better believe because I can't imagine what's happening with our child." Oh yes, there are children and youth reading this who are going to lead the way and see it. Praise God! So as you make your offering, you are pouring oil.

As you are reading this, what has been happening is an enlarging that has taken place on the inside of you, which has to happen before anything happens outside of you. There has been a stretching taking place. While you've been reading, some of you looked like gummy bears because you were being stretched. You are being stretched!

2. THE CONSECRATION

> I REALIZED THAT IT WASN'T ABOUT GOD'S WILL, IT WAS ABOUT ME BECOMING YIELDED, AND PLACING MYSELF INTO HIS HANDS.

Now before we go to communion, let's talk about the consecration that's needed, and this is the second part of making a vow. We've done the first part with the offering. I would say of everything we do when we run revival meetings, once a week, no matter where we are in the world, the service will be centered around consecration. Because when the Lord spoke to me about His will, I realized what that meant. I realized it wasn't about God's will. It was about me becoming yielded, and placing myself into His Hands.

Because a lot of people say, "Well, if the Lord wants to, He can do *this* or *that*," but God never overrides people's wills. He's given you a free will to decide. And some people decide not to do anything and some want to do this in a crowd, but this is not something you can do with a crowd, this is something you have to do individually.

Now go with me to Matthew 26:36-46. When you look at this passage of Scripture and realize this is Jesus praying, you wonder why Jesus would have to pray this. Wasn't it sufficient that He came to the Earth? Heaven knew He came and took on human flesh to go to the place called Calvary. So what is all this about? Was Jesus battling within Himself? Was Jesus struggling within Himself? No, He was setting an example for us. Everything we would face, He faced for us, and really, He showed us how to run the race. It's the consecrated life that's going to run the race. It is the consecrated and yielded vessel unto Him. And it's very interesting that this took place right after the woman broke the alabaster box of very precious perfume and poured it on His head.

So the consecration came right after the offering. And that's what I've found over the years—the offering resembles a tangible thing in the natural, but it's also the spiritual thing resulting in the consecration of the person. Somebody says, "Yes, but Jesus wasn't giving an offering." Yes He was, He was giving Himself. He was about to pour out Himself, just like the woman poured the perfume and took what was precious to her and poured it on Jesus. The fragrance filled the house, which was the house of Simon the leper and leprosy represents sin. But the perfume filled the house so you couldn't smell leprosy anymore. Lazarus who'd been dead was there, and the smell of death was blocked out, all because of a woman's gift.

The perfume was preparing Jesus for His burial so that even those who would then flog Him and beat Him, would smell the fragrance of the perfume—that offering that was poured on Jesus. They would smell the Rose of Sharon and the Lily of the Valley as the fragrance filled the courtyard that day as those Roman soldiers whipped Him and as His flesh flew through the air. But now in the Garden, Jesus has to come to the place where He's got to push right through, "I have to lay My life down. No one takes My life from Me. I lay it down and I have to trust My Father. This is a cup I have to drink for mankind, for the sin of the world. It's a bitter cup."

So if you look at verse 36, "Then cometh Jesus with them unto a place called Gethsemane, and saith unto the disciples, Sit ye here, while I go and pray yonder." I was thinking about this, He was already anointed now with the fragrance of the perfume, He was in Gethsemane, His attackers would come at Him, and they never would have smelt anybody like this before. Because there's a fragrance to the anointing.

When the anointing comes in a room, it changes everything. It changes *everything*. "And he took with him Peter and the two sons of Zebedee, and began to be sorrowful and very heavy" (v. 37). This is a struggle because you realize you are crossing over, maybe from one year to another, one season of your life to another, or figuratively, making the decision to leave the past behind and live consecrated unto Him and making the devil pay for what he has done in your life. Thank God, we don't do this drunk in the natural, we're just drunk in the Holy Ghost!

> Then saith he unto them, My soul is exceeding sorrowful, even unto death: tarry ye here, and watch with me. And he went a little further, and fell on his face, and prayed, saying, O my Father, if it be possible, let this cup pass from me: nevertheless not as I will, but as thou wilt.
>
> (VV. 38-39)

You have to do that today. Pray that prayer to tell the Lord, "Lord, whatever You have for me in the future, I want that. Not my will, but Thine be done." And maybe you find yourself between a rock and a hard place, because I know the struggle. I've been there, many, many times. There are things I'm believing God for right now that you could never believe

God for because you're not facing those things. There are things I'm expecting and believing God for that are going to impact multitudes of people. It doesn't affect you because you're not in that position that it would affect, but it will definitely affect your family and maybe some of your close friends right now. But the consecration nonetheless, is still the same.

> And he cometh unto the disciples, and findeth them asleep, and saith unto Peter, What, could ye not watch with me one hour?
>
> (V. 40)

That's always the hardest thing—coming into that place where the people who are the closest to you are snoring, "Oh, great! Here I am in the fight of my life and these guys are sleeping." They're asleep and snoring. He came to His disciples and found them asleep and said, "Peter, could you not watch with me for one hour? Couldn't you just pray for one hour?" But Peter is gone, fast asleep.

> Watch and pray, that ye enter not into temptation: the spirit indeed is willing, but the flesh is weak.
>
> (V. 41)

We see that during the all-night prayer meetings. There are people who come, bless their hearts, and they lie down on the chairs. Then we'll walk around at 2:00 a.m. and you can hear snoring coming from the pews! And they are not groaning in the spirit, it's just the flesh. The spirit was willing, but the flesh was weak, and the flesh went to sleep!

He went away again the second time, and prayed, saying, O my Father, if this cup may not pass away from me, except I drink it, thy will be done.

(V. 42)

In other words, there was no other way. There was *no other way*. He was now complying to the will of God because it was God's plan from before the foundation of the world, that He was the Lamb slain, and He was now going to Calvary. That's the reason why He came, He was born to die. And now, He was there to fill the Heavenly obligation that would satisfy the courts of Heaven.

And he came and found them asleep again: for their eyes were heavy. And he left them, and went away again, and prayed the third time, saying the same words. Then cometh he to his disciples, and saith unto them, Sleep on now, and take your rest: behold, the hour is at hand, and the Son of man is betrayed into the hands of sinners. Rise, let us be going: behold, he is at hand that doth betray me.

(VV. 43-46)

This is very interesting because one minute it was, "All right, go ahead and sleep," but then the next "Get up, because here comes Judas."

Here comes Judas who was provoked into betraying Jesus, based on the gift of a woman who brought her alabaster box of precious perfume that was equivalent to one year's salary. And Judas turned around and sold Jesus for $21.70. So you will either worship Him, or you will sell Him! And right after that, was the total betrayal, the arrest, going before Caiaphas, and

Peter denying Him. Even Peter, who fell asleep, denied him. And then Judas felt sorry for what he did and tried to give it back. But they wouldn't take it back, so he hanged himself. And then you see the struggle—Jesus mocked by the soldiers and then the crucifixion and all that took place there.

> YOU WILL EITHER WORSHIP HIM, OR YOU WILL SELL HIM!

LAYING EVERYTHING ON THE ALTAR
Now when I talk along these lines, immediately people think, *Well, are you referring to me dying?* No. Yet it could be that several of us will pay the price for the Gospel with our lives. You ask, "What are you talking about?" Because of where you travel; because of where you go. But that's not even something you think about. That's something you resolve within yourself.

I remember several years ago, we were up in Connecticut, and I went to Yale University. This University was built by one of the great revivalists. As I went to the library, right before you enter the library in the main hall was a huge painting of a gentleman. I read the footnotes on the painting which was from 1896. This man was a graduate of Yale University and it said, "This is in memory of this gentleman who gave his life in China. He was one of the first martyrs out of Yale University." And there it was still today, in that Great Hall in Yale, which is probably one of the most godless, heathen institutions on the planet.

And with what is coming over the next five to ten years, there might be a place we build that will actually have pictures of the martyrs who will come out of R.M.I. You say, "What are you talking about, Pastor?" I'll just go back to 2004/2005 when Reinhard Bonnke was preaching at the graduation of the River Bible Institute. He turned to me and said, "Rodney, I feel I am standing here with the first wave of end-time martyrs of the Church," and he said, "I've never felt that anywhere in the world until I came here to The River."

Now suddenly, the atmosphere changes—*I'm not too sure I want to consecrate myself. What are you talking about, Pastor?* I'm talking about *everything* on the line. I'm talking about laying *everything* on the altar—your life, your breath. This is not a game. We're not playing church. This is a matter of life and death. Someone says, "Yes, but I'm not required to walk that way." When you are a child of God, you do not designate anything.

Because the enemies of the Cross of Jesus Christ don't care what you are. They don't care if you are Methodist, Presbyterian, Baptist, Charismatic, Pentecostal, or you just live on a farm. If you believe in the Cross of Jesus Christ, you are an enemy. You are an infidel and you must die.

Someone says, "Well, we're not like you, you speak in tongues." It doesn't matter. Tongue talkers and non-tongue talkers will die all the same because the attack is against the Cross of Jesus Christ. That's why in consecration, we even did this with our own children. In 1993, when we moved into our new home that was built in the New Tampa area, Adonica and I sat our three children (Kirsten, Kelly and Kenneth) down, and said, "This house is only ours for a season. The day might come when they come and take it away from us and tell us that we have to denounce Jesus." And we looked at the children and said, "You will never denounce Jesus. You will say, 'Go ahead.' And they might even separate us and say, 'We're going to kill your mother and father in front of you.' And they might even say to us, 'We're going to kill your children in front of you.' And we'll say to you, 'We love you. We'll see you on the other side,' but we will *never, ever* denounce Jesus."

And it is easy to agree with that now, but when it's your own child that's ripped from your arms, then you'll realize whether you are consecrated or not.

What you don't even realize is that over the last 10-12 years, there have been many days when I have said goodbye to Adonica and I did not know if I would see her again. And every time I see my kids, I kiss them as though it is the last time I'll ever see them, and my grandbabies the same. Because I realize I'm not backing down. I will never compromise what I'm preaching, and I understand the ultimate price might be my life. But if it means death, then so be it. We will *never* compromise.

Even that morning of my arrest, I did not know what would take place. Under the Patriot Act, the most damnable document ever signed in recent history by George W. Bush, every right of every citizen of this nation is taken away. So they can arrest you, put you away without a trial, and make you disappear. So I didn't know if I'd ever see Adonica and the family again. I thought, *This is it. They're going to make me go "bye-bye."* But I had a total peace. I looked at Adonica and I said, "I love you so much. I never thought it would come to this. But tell everybody I send my love." Now it didn't turn out like that at all. As you know, I went in to the jail for 40 minutes and then fell asleep in the cell because I was tired. There was nobody there. The prison had been emptied to make room for the preachers! All the criminals were roaming the streets and I had the whole prison to myself—all 17 cells! I even walked in there and said, "So where do you want me?" "Anywhere will do." "This one looks good. I'll pick this one." But I did not know if I would see Adonica again.

And you have to come to that place. I'm not asking anybody to die reading this. I'm trying to talk to you about consecration. What is consecration? It's placing *everything* on the altar. So today, as we consecrate ourselves afresh, not to *our* will, not to *our* plan, not to *our* purpose, but to *His* will, we can celebrate knowing our life is in His Hands. We have nothing to lose. We have *nothing* to lose. Absolutely nothing, because eternal life is already ours.

They might kill your body, but they can't kill *you*. I know there are people reading this who will say, "Pastor, this will never happen in America." Well, go back 10 years and they would have said, "There'll never be a day they arrest a pastor for keeping the church open." But it happened. You may say, "Well, there'll never be a day when they execute people in America." Oh, really? Why is it that our brothers and sisters in the Middle East, in China, and in other parts of the world, give their lives for the Gospel, and Americans close their church on a Sunday so people can spend more time with their children?

Why is that? Because God's Word is not honored, and God is not respected. God is not honored as He should be. He's just treated as "a thing that people do." So I'm going to lead you in a prayer of consecration today, and then into communion. I'm not asking you to die, I'm asking you to live. We actually need you living, we don't need you dead. There's a saying, "Dead men tell no tales," but dead men don't preach either! It takes somebody who's alive and breathing, and has the breath of God in their lungs. That's who will carry this Gospel to the far-flung corners of the globe. It's those who have counted the cost—whatever that might be.

So write down what you are believing God for these upcoming years and I want you to be exact. I want you to be specific. The things you write must come from your heart. The Lord sees, hears, and the Lord knows. Then hold this list in your hands. Let's pray and then I'm going to lead you in consecration, followed by communion.

THE PRAYER OF CONSECRATION

Father, as Your people hold in their hands, the things they are believing You for, things to do in the natural and things pertaining to their personal life. As singles, young people, children, teenagers, parents, married couples, single moms, business people, men and woman, ministers of the Gospel that function in every one of the offices, and people who are operating in different realms and spheres, we hold these things in our hand even now, that represent even the deepest desires and the cries of the hearts of Your people. And today, by way of consecration, as You look down upon each person, that in the Name that is above every name, the Name of Jesus, You meet them at the point of their need, and the cry of their heart. And today, what is written down here is sealed.

Father, what is written down in accordance with Your plan and purpose for their life, it shall come to pass. Forbid that anyone should write that their dream is a death of someone—may that not come to pass. Forbid that people would have written one thing that would be amiss. But those things that have been written that are pure, that are true, that are holy, by way of consecration this day, we surrender to You and we place it on the altar. That these next 12 months, we will see this come to pass in their life. And Lord, we are going to ask that it'll happen speedily. That Lord, some of the things that they've written out, even by the end of next month, should already be in place and by the next five months, Lord, let some of these things be moved so supernaturally that by the end of the seventh month, they'll have to make another list, because You'll have already done super-abundantly above all that they could even ask or think. We are asking that El-Shaddai will step into the middle of this and cause it, and grant it, to come to pass. And Lord, that You'll speak to them in the night hour. You'll speak to them dreams, You'll speak to them and show them exactly what to do. And then they'll get up in the day and will execute exactly that. Not our will but Yours be done. And we pray this now, in Jesus' Name.

Now just raise one of your hands to Heaven and pray this after me by way of consecration:

Pray this out loud:

Father, today I surrender my life afresh to You. Not my will but Yours be done. Today, I confess Jesus is my Lord and my Savior. Today, my life does not belong to me, but it belongs to You. I'll go where You want me to go. I'll do what You want me to do. I'll say what You want me to say, and I'll be what You want me to be. Not my will, but Yours be done. Jesus, You are my Lord and my Savior. What I've written down is from my heart, and I present it to You and I lay it on the altar. Have Your way in me, do whatever you want. I'm Yours. I belong to You. Take me, I come as I am. And I yield myself to You. From this night, I will follow You. From this day I will live a pure life. From this day I will live, by Your grace, a holy life and I'm going to serve You every day of my life. With every fiber of my being and with all of my strength, I'll serve You. My life is not mine, my life is Yours. Use me. I'm Yours. Lord, I yield myself even now, afresh.

Now, lift your hands and just begin to thank Him right now.

Now Lord, because this is an altar and every one of Your altars involve fire, I'm asking now that the fire come now in Jesus' Name on every person, from the top of their head to the very soles of their feet. Seal this even now. Explode things on the inside of Your people, Lord. Amen.

Let the fire of God fall on the altar of your heart right now. As you have poured out the oil today, the Lord is pouring out the oil on you. He's not only pouring out the oil, He's pouring out the wine right now. Drink. Drink. Drink. Drink, of the new wine. Drink, Vino nuevos. The Hand of the Lord is touching people right now.

3. COMMUNION

Now to communion, the third part of the vow. Wherever you are, I want you to go and get the communion elements and have them ready to partake.

Now don't think you get anything from God because you have earned it! It's this Table of the Lord that has carried us, especially in the past three years, and it is this Table that will carry us through the years to come.

This Table represents the Body that was broken, bruised, and torn for you, and the Blood that was shed for you. That by the stripes of Jesus, you *were* healed. That's what the scripture says in 1 Peter 2:24. And by the Blood, your sins are washed away and you are sealed. When we seal foods in Operation Eden here at R.M.I., we make sure there's no air in there. We vacuum pack it and we seal it. And when you get sealed by the Blood, nothing can get in you. You are sealed by the Blood to the day of redemption. It's the Blood that keeps you holy. It's the Blood that keeps you pure. It's the Blood that protects you so that no harm and evil can come nigh to you, all because of the Blood.

Isaiah 53:4-5:

Surely he hath borne our griefs, and carried our sorrows: yet we did esteem him stricken, smitten of God, and afflicted. But he was wounded for our transgressions, he was bruised for our iniquities: the chastisement of our peace was upon him; and with his stripes we are healed.

Matthew 8:17:

That it might be fulfilled which was spoken by Esaias the prophet, saying, Himself took our infirmities, and bare our sicknesses.

1 Peter 2:24:

Who his own self bare our sins in his own body on the tree, that we, being dead to sins, should live unto righteousness: by whose stripes ye were healed.

So Father, we hold this bread in our hands, symbolic of the Body of Jesus, and as we take of this bread and place it in our mouth, we are quickened and made whole. We promise we will break this bread to a lost and dying world, and we will never keep it to ourselves. We forgive everyone who has ever hurt us, even as You forgive us. And we receive this now by faith in Jesus' Name.

This cup, this Blood, is so precious. This Blood that joins us together with Him. That today, from every tribe and tongue and from many nationalities, we've all been made one because of Your Blood. The Blood for one is the Blood for all. Your Blood is holy and Your Blood is pure. And Your Blood keeps us holy, Your Blood keeps us pure, Your Blood carries us until we see You face to face, and Your Blood protects us. We receive this now by faith, in Jesus' Name.

In the world they drink, but they are not getting like Jesus. They are getting filled with rubbish. The more of Him that we drink, the more like Him we become. It's drinking not thinking. Some of you are trying to drink by thinking. You can't drink thinking. You drink with your heart. It's called joy—ha, ha, ha. The Holy Spirit is all around us, "Filling our hearts with His joy. Jump into the river and drink from the well, springing up from the fountain of the Holy Ghost" ("There's a New Wine," Stacey Swalley).

Pray for the world, it's going to be rough the upcoming years. For you, it's going to be okay. For the consecrated ones, the yielded ones, it is going to be great. For everybody else, it's going to be pretty much hell. Aren't you glad that you're redeemed and you're washed in His Blood? Amen!

So as I conclude this book, remember that making a vow is a holy and precious thing before the Lord and not to be done lightly. It's where you lay your life down and say, "Everything I have, and everything I am, is Yours." Because once you have made a vow, you can get up every day and do only what He tells you to do, based on that vow. You'll decree, and then it will happen and what God will do for you, history will be written about. People will be amazed and ask you, "How are you doing what you are doing?" And you will reply, "It's a place called 'a vow.'"

> IT'S THE CONSECRATED LIFE THAT'S GOING TO RUN THE RACE. IT IS THE CONSECRATED AND YIELDED VESSEL UNTO HIM.

Things God Has Spoken to Me Over the Past Three Years:

_____

_____

_____

_____

Things I am believing God for:

_____

_____

_____

_____

_____

Date:_____ Time:_____

My Offering:

_____

_____

_____

_____

_____

_____

_____

_____

_____

_____

_____

_____

_____

*Date:*_____ *Time:*_____

My Vow:

_____

_____

_____

_____

_____

_____

_____

_____

_____

_____

_____

_____

*Date:*_____ *Time:*_____

POSTSCRIPT

If you have been blessed and challenged by this book, please write to us here at our Tampa office or email us at testimonies@revival.com.

We would love to hear from you. If you were stirred up and challenged to change and allow God to do His work in you, we pray that God would use you in a wonderful way to touch a lost and dying world.

Write to:
Revival Ministries International
P.O. Box 292888 Tampa, FL 33687

You can also reach us at www.revival.com/prayer/testimony
or
call 1(813) 971-9999

For souls and another Great Spiritual Awakening in America,
—DR. RODNEY HOWARD-BROWNE

ABOUT THE AUTHOR

Drs. Rodney and Adonica Howard-Browne are the founders of Revival Ministries International, the River at Tampa Bay Church, and River University in Tampa, Florida.

In December of 1987, Rodney, along with his wife, Adonica, and their three children, Kirsten, Kelly, and Kenneth, moved from their native land, South Africa, to the United States called by God as missionaries from Africa to America. The Lord had spoken through Rodney in a word of prophecy and declared, "As America has sown missionaries over the last two hundred years, I am going to raise up people from other nations to come to the United States of America. I am sending a mighty revival to America."

In April of 1989, the Lord sent a revival of signs and wonders and miracles that began in a church in Clifton Park, New York, that has continued until today, resulting in thousands of people being touched and changed as they encounter the presence of the living God. God is still moving today—saving, healing, delivering, restoring, and setting free!

Drs. Rodney and Adonica's second daughter, Kelly, was born with an incurable lung disease called cystic fibrosis. This demonic disease slowly destroyed her lungs. Early on Christmas morning 2002, at the age of eighteen, she ran out of lung capacity and

ABOUT THE AUTHOR

breathed out her last breath. They placed her into the arms of her Lord and Savior and then vowed a vow. First, they vowed that the devil would pay for what he had done to their family. Secondly, they vowed to do everything in their power, with the help of the Lord, to win one hundred million souls to Jesus and to put $1 billion into world missions and the harvest of souls.

When Drs. Rodney and Adonica became naturalized citizens of the United States of America, in 2008 and 2004 respectively, they took the United States Oath of Allegiance, which declares, "I will support and defend the Constitution and laws of the United States of America against all enemies, foreign and domestic." They took this oath to heart. They love America, are praying for this country, and are trusting God to see another Great Awakening sweep across this land.

Believing for this Great Spiritual Awakening, Drs. Rodney and Adonica conducted Celebrate America D.C., a soul winning event. They preached the Gospel of Jesus Christ for fifty nights in Washington, D.C., and surrounding areas from 2014 to 2019. Through the evangelism efforts on the streets, in the halls of Congress, and the nightly altar calls, 58,033 individuals made decisions for Jesus Christ.

During Celebrate America, in July of 2014, at the Daughters of the American Revolution Constitution Hall, Dr. Rodney executed a restraining order against the structure that is holding America in captivity, binding it and rendering it powerless and ineffective, from the Supreme Court, to the White House, to the Executive Branch, Congress, and the Senate, in the Name of Jesus. He commanded the Church in America to wake up and for the people of God to come out of their slumber. He declared that it is time to take the land.

During the Covid era, Drs. Rodney and Adonica took a

ABOUT THE AUTHOR

stand for the Gospel of Jesus Christ. As a result, Dr. Rodney was wrongfully arrested at his home on March 30, 2020, for holding a church service at The River at Tampa Bay Church on Sunday, March 29.

As a result of his arrest, Florida Governor Ron DeSantis declared attendance at churches, synagogues, and houses of worship to be an essential activity. Dr. Rodney's arrest freed up every church in Florida to meet. All the charges were dropped by the Thirteenth Judicial Circuit State Attorney on May 15, 2020, and the date of his arrest and criminal record were expunged by Circuit Court Judge John N. Conrad on February 22, 2021.

Drs. Rodney and Adonica continue to take a stand for the Word of God and for billions around the world whose right to worship freely was removed and has not been, or perhaps will never be, restored. The Stand nightly services have continued for over 1,300 nights, as they stand for their brothers and sisters around the world who cannot stand freely.

With a passion for souls and a passion to revive and mobilize the Body of Christ, Drs. Rodney and Adonica have conducted revivals and soul winning efforts throughout ninety-two nations with the 300 City Tour, Good News campaigns, R.M.I. Revivals, the Great Awakening Tours, and The Stand. As a result, over 47,694,747 precious people have come to Christ, and tens of thousands of believers have been revived and mobilized to preach the Gospel of Jesus Christ. For more information, visit revival.com.

CONNECT

Please visit revival.com or rodneyhowardbrowne.com for our latest updates and news. Many of our services are live online. Additionally, many of our recorded services are available on Video on Demand.

For a listing of Drs. Rodney and Adonica Howard-Browne's products and itinerary, please visit revival.com. To download the soul-winning tools for free, please visit revival.com and click on Soul-winning Tools.

- **Like us on Facebook:**
  Facebook.com/rodneyadonicahowardbrowne

- **Follow us on X:**
  @rhowardbrowne

- **Follow us on YouTube:**
  YouTube.com/rodneyhowardbrowne

- **Follow us on Instagram:**
  @rodneyhowardbrowne

- **Follow us on Rumble:**
  @rhowardbrowne

OTHER BOOKS AND RESOURCES
BY RODNEY HOWARD-BROWNE

BOOKS
The Ways of the Wind
The Holy Spirit
Revival
Communion: The Table
　of the Lord
The Call of God
Kingdom Business
Leadership Principles
The Phantom Virus
Socialism Under the Microscope
God's Top Ten
Perpetual Harvest
Killing the Planet: How
　a Financial Cartel
　Doomed Mankind
The Anointing
The Killing of Uncle of Sam:
　The Demise of the United
　States of America
Thoughts on Stewardship
The Coming Revival
The Touch of God
The Gifts of the Holy Spirit
The Reality of Life After Death
Seeing Jesus as He Really Is
The Curse Is Not Greater than
　the Blessing
How to Increase and Release
　the Anointing
School of the Spirit
Manifesting the Holy Ghost

OTHER BOOKS AND RESOURCES BY RODNEY HOWARD-BROWNE

What Gifts Do You
 Bring the King?
Prayer Journal
Sowing in Famine

AUDIO CDS
Prayer Time
Weapons of Our Warfare
Becoming One Flesh
Faith
Flowing in the Holy Ghost
How to Flow in the Anointing
Igniting the Fire
In Search of the Anointing
Prayer that Moves Mountains
Accelerate
The Camels are Coming
Pray Without Ceasing Vol.1
Pray Without Ceasing Vol.2
The Touch of God
Mountain Moving Prayer
Having an Encounter with God
God's Mandate
The Anointing is Transferable
Dealing with Offenses
The Vow and the Decree
Whosoever Can Get Whatsoever
Run to the Water
Demonstrations of the Spirit
 and of Power
The Double Portion
More Than Laughter
The Hand of the Lord

Running the Heavenly Race
The Holy Spirit, His
 Purpose & Power
The Power to Create Wealth
Walking in Heaven's Light
All These Blessings
A Surplus of Prosperity
The Joy of the Lord is
 My Strength
Prayer Secrets
Communion–The Table
 of the Lord
My Roadmap
My Mission–My Purpose
My Heart
My Family
My Worship
Decreeing Faith
Ingredients of Revival
Fear Not
Matters of the Heart by Dr.
 Adonica Howard-Browne
My Treasure
My Absolutes
My Father
My Crowns
My Comforter & Helper
Renewing the Mind
Seated in High Places
Triumphant Entry
Merchandising and Trafficking
 the Anointing
My Prayer Life

OTHER BOOKS AND RESOURCES BY RODNEY HOWARD-BROWNE

My Jesus
Seeing Jesus as He Really Is
Exposing the World's System
Living in the Land of
  Visions & Dreams
Kingdom Business
Taking Cities in the
  Land of Giants
Spiritual Hunger
The Two Streams

MP3 CDS
The Phantom Virus
Socialism Under the Microscope
Killing the Planet: How
  a Financial Cartel
  Doomed Mankind
The Killing of Uncle Sam
The Touch of God:
  The Anointing
Knowing the Person of the
  Holy Spirit
The Love Walk
How to Hear the Voice of God
Matters of the Heart
Exposing the World's System
How to Be Led by the Holy Spirit
The Anointing
The Ways of the Wind

DVDS
Mountain Moving Prayer
How to Personally Lead
  Someone to Jesus

The Fire of God
Vision for America
Living the Christian Lifestyle
No Limits No Boundaries
The Curse is Not Greater Than
  the Blessing
God's Glory Manifested through
  Special Anointings
Good News New York
Jerusalem Ablaze
The Mercy of God by Dr.
  Adonica Howard-Browne
Are You a Performer or
  a Minister?
Revival at ORU
  Volume 1, 2 & 3
The Realms of God
Singapore Ablaze
The Coat My Father Gave Me
Have You Ever Wondered What
  Jesus Was Like?
There Is a Storm Coming
  (Recorded live from
  Good News New York)
Budapest, Hungary Ablaze
The Camels Are Coming
Power Evangelism
Taking Cities in the
  Land of Giants
Renewing the Mind
Triumphant Entry
Merchandising and Trafficking
  the Anointing

OTHER BOOKS AND RESOURCES BY RODNEY HOWARD-BROWNE

Doing Business with God
Accelerate

MUSIC
Nothing Is Impossible
By His Stripes
Run with Fire
The Sweet Presence of Jesus
Eternity with Kelly Howard-Browne
Live from the River
You're Such a Good God to Me
Howard-Browne Family Christmas

He Lives
Anointed—The Decade of the '80s
Live Summer Campmeeting '15
Live Summer Campmeeting '16
Haitian Praise
No Limits
Christmas Extravaganza At The River Vol. 1 & 2
The Stand
Youth Week EP
Kids Week EP

THE RIVER AT TAMPA BAY CHURCH

The River at Tampa Bay Church was founded on December 1, 1996. At the close of 1996, the Lord planted within Pastors Rodney and Adonica's heart the vision and desire to start a church in Tampa. With a heart for the lost and to minister to those who had been touched by revival, they implemented that vision and began The River at Tampa Bay, with the motto, "Church with a Difference."

Over 575 people joined them for the first Sunday morning service on December 1, 1996. Over the years, the membership has grown and the facilities have changed, yet these three things have remained constant since the church's inception ... dynamic praise and worship, anointed preaching and teaching of the Word, and powerful demonstrations of the Holy Spirit and power. The Lord spoke to Pastor Rodney's heart to feed the people, touch the people, and love the people. With this in mind and heart, the goal of The River is:

To become a model revival church where people from all over the world can come and be touched by God. Once they have been not only touched, but changed, they are ready to be launched out into the harvest field with the anointing of God.

To have a church that is multi-racial, representing a cross

section of society from rich to poor from all nations, bringing people to a place of maturity in their Christian walk.

To see the lost, the backslidden and the unsure come to a full assurance of their salvation.

To be a home base for Revival Ministries International and all of its arms. A base offering strength and support to the vision of R.M.I. to see America shaken with the fires of revival, then to take that fire to the far-flung corners of the globe.

To break the mold of religious tradition and thinking.

To be totally dependent upon the Holy Spirit for His leading and guidance as we lead others deeper into the River of God.

Our motto: Church with a Difference.

For The River at Tampa Bay's service times and directions, please, visit revival.com or call (813) 971-9999. Location: The River at Tampa Bay Church, 3738 River International Dr., Tampa, FL 33610.

RIVER UNIVERSITY

River University is a place where men and women of all ages, backgrounds, and experiences can gather together to study and experience the glory of God. River University is not a traditional Bible school. It is a Holy Ghost training center, birthed specifically for those whose strongest desire is to know Christ and to make Him known.

The vision for River University is plain: To train men and women in the spirit of revival for ministry in the 21st century. The school was birthed in 1997, with a desire to train up revivalists for the 21st century. It is a place where the Word of God and the Holy Spirit come together to produce life, birth ministries, and launch them out. River University is a place where ministries are sent to the far-flung corners of the globe to spread revival, and to bring in a harvest of souls for the Kingdom of God.

While preaching in many nations and regions of the world, Dr. Rodney Howard-Browne has observed that all the people of the earth have one thing in common: a desperate need for the genuine touch of God. From the interior of Alaska through the bush country of Africa, to the outback villages of Australia, to the cities of North America, people are tired of religion and ritualistic worship. They are crying out for the reality of His presence. River University is dedicated to training believers how to live, minister, and flow in the anointing.

The Word will challenge those attending to find clarity in their calling, and be changed by the awesome presence of God. This is the hour of God's power, not just for the full-time minister, but for all of God's people who are hungry for more. Whether you are a housewife or an aspiring evangelist, River University will deepen your relationship and experience in the Lord, and provide you with a new perspective on how to reach others with God's life-changing power.

Programs Include:

- River Bible Institute

- River School of Worship

- River School of Government

- River Bible Español

You can be saturated in the Word and the Spirit of God at River University. Since 1997, River University has graduated over 10,159 students (including our subsidiary schools). River University is the place where you will be empowered to reach your high calling and set your world on fire with revival. For more information about River University, please visit revival.com, or call (813) 899-0085 or (813) 971-9999.

RIVER SCHOOL OF THE BIBLE ONLINE

River School of the Bible is our online school to train up revivalists for the 21st century. It was started so that those who are unable to come to the school in Tampa, can receive this training and impartation, anyplace worldwide. It is not a traditional Bible school. It is a Holy Ghost training center, birthed specifically for those whose strongest desire is to know Christ and to make Him known.

This program provides quality, Spirit-filled Biblical instruction, academic training, and practical education to men and women called into the five-fold ministry, or for those who desire to become better equipped in other areas of Christian service. Since 2018, over 100 students have graduated from the school. So, don't wait! God wants to raise you up to do great things for Him.

For more information, please visit revival.com/rsb, or email rsb@revival.com

GOD WANTS TO USE YOU TO BRING IN THE HARVEST OF SOULS!

The Great Commission, "Go ye into all the world and preach the Gospel to every creature," is for every believer to take personally. Every believer is to be an announcer of the Good News Gospel. When the Gospel is preached, people have an encounter with Jesus. Jesus is the only One Who can change the heart of a man, woman, child, and nation!

On the next page is a tool to assist you in sharing the Gospel with others. It is called, "The Gospel Soul-Winning Script." Please make copies of it, fold it in the center lengthwise, and read it to people. As you read it to others, you will see many come to Christ, because as stated in Romans 1:16, *"For I am not ashamed of the gospel of Christ: for it is the power of God unto salvation to every one that believeth ..."*

Please visit revival.com, click on Soul-Winning Tools, and review the many tools and videos that are freely available to help you bring in the harvest of souls. It is harvest time!

THE GOSPEL SOUL-WINNING — SCRIPT —

Has anyone ever told you that God loves you and that He has a wonderful plan for your life? I have a real quick, but important question to ask you. If you were to die this very second, do you know for sure, beyond a shadow of a doubt, that you would go to Heaven? [If "Yes"— Great, why would you say "Yes"? (If they respond with anything but "I have Jesus in my heart" or something similar to that, PROCEED WITH SCRIPT) or "No" or "I hope so" PROCEED WITH SCRIPT.]

Let me quickly share with you what the Holy Bible reads. It reads "for all have sinned and come short of the glory of God" and "for the wages of sin is death, but the gift of God is eternal life through Jesus Christ our Lord". The Bible also reads, "For whosoever shall call upon the name of the Lord shall be saved". And you're a "whosoever" right? Of course you are; all of us are.

continued on reverse side—

I'm going to say a quick prayer for you. Lord, bless (FILL IN NAME) and his/her family with long and healthy lives. Jesus, make Yourself real to him/her and do a quick work in his/her heart. If (FILL IN NAME) has not received Jesus Christ as his/her Lord and Savior, I pray he/she will do so now.

(FILL IN NAME), if you would like to receive the gift that God has for you today, say this after me with your heart and lips out loud. Dear Lord Jesus, come into my heart. Forgive me of my sin. Wash me and cleanse me. Set me free. Jesus, thank You that You died for me. I believe that You are risen from the dead and that You're coming back again for me. Fill me with the Holy Spirit. Give me a passion for the lost, a hunger for the things of God and a holy boldness to preach the gospel of Jesus Christ. I'm saved; I'm born again, I'm forgiven and I'm on my way to Heaven because I have Jesus in my heart.

As a minister of the gospel of Jesus Christ, I tell you today that all of your sins are forgiven. Always remember to run to God and not from God because He loves you and has a great plan for your life.

[Invite them to your church and get follow up info: name, address, & phone number.]

Revival Ministries International
P.O. Box 292888 • Tampa, FL 33687
(813) 971-9999 • www.revival.com

THE RIVER AT TAMPA BAY CHURCH
ALTAR CALL

CELEBRATE AMERICA
WASHINGTON, D.C.
57,498 SALVATIONS

THE STAND | 1,300 NIGHTS AND COUNTING

THE GREAT AWAKENING BROADCAST WITH
CHRISTIAN TELEVISION NETWORK
OVER 42 MILLION RECORDED DECISIONS FOR CHRIST

GOOD NEWS NEW YORK - 1999
MADISON SQUARE GARDEN
48,459 SALVATIONS

GOOD NEWS NEW YORK - 1999
MADISON SQUARE GARDEN
48,459 SALVATIONS

GOOD NEW SOWETO - 2004
SOWETO, SOUTH AFRICA
177,600 SALVATIONS

GOOD NEWS UMLAZI - 2005
UMLAZI, SOUTH AFRICA
286,750 SALVATIONS

SINGAPORE - 1995

THE EARLY YEARS
RODNEY, ADONICA, KIRSTEN, KELLY, & KENNETH

THE EARLY YEARS
RODNEY & ADONICA